THE POLYTUNNEL BOOK

FRUIT AND VEGETABLES ALL YEAR ROUND

THE POLYTUNNEL BOOK

FRUIT AND VEGETABLES ALL YEAR ROUND

JOYCE RUSSELL

PHOTOGRAPHS BY
BEN RUSSELL

F

FRANCES LINCOLN LIMITED
PUBLISHERS

For my sister Helen

Frances Lincoln Limited
4 Torriano Mews
Torriano Avenue
London NW5 2RZ
www.franceslincoln.com

The Polytunnel Book
Copyright © Frances Lincoln Limited 2011
Text copyright © Joyce Russell 2011
Photographs copyright © Ben Russell 2011
First Frances Lincoln edition 2011

A catalogue record for this book is available from the British Library.

ISBN 978-0-7112-3170-2

Printed and bound in China

9 8 7 6 5 4 3 2 1

CONTENTS

INTRODUCTION

I bought a polytunnel about sixteen years ago. It seemed like a major investment at the time and, with a large garden already growing a wide range of crops, I wasn't sure how much use it would be. By the first summer I was so passionate about polytunnel growing that when winter came along I simply couldn't stop. Boundaries have to be pushed, and I wanted to see if it would be possible to keep the polytunnel cropping all year round. In the years since then, I have lost none of that passion. I've learned more and more about how to make an ordinary-sized polytunnel provide enough food to keep a family eating through winter and summer alike; and I've enjoyed, every day, excellent fruit and vegetables that have to travel only a few strides from the plant to the plate.

A polytunnel is a wonderful thing! It costs a fraction of the price of a traditional glass greenhouse and it's put up quickly to cover a large space. It provides a warmer environment than the great outdoors; it blocks wind and shelters from rain. Tender crops that would have difficulty growing outside thrive in it and the gardener thrives too when working in, and reaping the rewards of, such a protected space.

Maybe enthusiasts tend to go on about their passions, but at least I found an outlet for mine over the years in writing features for garden magazines. Gardeners are inventive people. They are people who like to do the best they can with whatever resources come

to hand. But most of all they like to share their tips (and their problems) and to encourage new growers to become part of the gardening clan.

This book is born of a need to share. It's born of readers asking when I'm going to put a book together to save them time hunting through back issues of magazines. It's also born of the questions of my gardening friends, who phone or email at regular intervals to ask: 'Is it time to sow basil?' 'My cucumber plants have flopped. What can I do?' Or, most of all: 'What should I be doing in the polytunnel now?'

That last question was my starting point. This book is designed to provide some answers as it guides the reader through the growing year in an unheated polytunnel. I hope it also inspires people to experiment and to continue the tradition of sharing their tips, troubles and triumphs with other gardeners. But most of all, I hope this book helps readers to develop a passion for growing great polytunnel crops.

HOW TO USE THIS BOOK

There's a lot of information contained within these pages. Some of this will be more suited to the beginner grower and some will be more appropriate for the experienced gardener. Flick through the pages and get a feel for things. Learn how to use the book, so that it gives you what you want. And don't worry if it gets a little grubby from constant use.

PART 1 explains how to choose, put up and lay out a polytunnel. It also tackles the issue of planning permission. In all cases, this section is only a guide. It's always best to ask the experts if you can. Each individual manufacturer will give the best instructions for their own particular structure and some of these will put it up for you if you want.

PART 2 lists some tools and supplies that you might find useful.

PART 3 is a month-by-month guide to polytunnel growing. Each month has a list of jobs that can be done. There's also a list of fruit, vegetables or herbs that can be sown. These are suggestions and the text for each month gives more detail and a scattering of interesting tips. It's probably best to read the bit about sowing carrots in January if it's the first time you've considered making such an early sowing. If you've made similar sowings in previous years, however, the list might be enough to act as a memory prod.

PART 4 gives an 'at a glance' overview of each of the main fruits and vegetables that can be grown in a polytunnel. If you want a quick reminder of the planting distance for aubergines, or when to reduce watering for pepper plants, this is the place to look. If you want to know more, this section will refer you to the relevant month.

PART 5 deals with pests and diseases. If there's a problem in the polytunnel, look here to find out what it might be. Don't despair! There are always solutions to problems and this section can help you negotiate the worst pitfalls.

PART 6 goes a little beyond the immediacy of month-by-month growing and looks at the overall plan. Get crop rotations organized, look after the soil and look after the structure of the polytunnel, and you should grow great crops for years to come.

PART 7 is for those who like to 'make their own' if they possibly can. There are recipes for potting compost, as well as how to set up a hotbed and how to make liquid feeds.

The list of suppliers shows just how easy it is to find someone to sell you a polytunnel, or seeds, or the pots, feeds and biological pest controls that can make it all come together as a perfectly functioning system.

☑ **The best tip:** get sowing, get growing, but most of all enjoy the delights of producing fruit and vegetables in a polytunnel all year round.

1

SETTING UP A POLYTUNNEL

CHOOSING THE RIGHT LOCATION

If there is only one place where the polytunnel will fit in the garden, that's where it goes and you have to cope with any faults of the site. If there is a choice, however, it's worth considering a few factors before settling on the final position.

How visible will the polytunnel be?

Polytunnels aren't beautiful things. If you have the option of putting one where it is hidden from view, this makes a lot of sense. Bear in mind that neighbours don't want it blocking a view any more than you do. Polytunnels come in different heights – a low one may be more discreet than a taller one.

How close to the house?

Try to choose a site close enough to the house so that popping out to open a door or pick veg isn't a daunting prospect, but not so close that it spoils the view.

Does the polytunnel have shelter from prevailing winds?

Avoid having a door opening pointed towards prevailing winds. If the wind blows straight in and can't get out, one gale can destroy the lot.

On exposed sites a bit of shelter is a good idea. A hedge can be kept trimmed so that it doesn't block light but still provides some protection. Large trees aren't such a good idea: they will overshadow the tunnel when in leaf, and falling branches can cause structural damage. It's also worth noting that roots from nearby trees will soon find their way into the enriched soil of the polytunnel. Windbreak netting can be put up alongside the polytunnel to provide extra protection.

What about shade?

Most polytunnel plants like sun and some will be slow to ripen if they don't get enough. In theory it's best to get as much sunlight as possible into the structure. In practice, most sites have some shaded spots at different times of the day. Aim to put the tunnel up where it gets sun for most of the day. If necessary, you can provide shade in other ways (by growing curtains of climbing beans, for example).

Should the ridge run north to south, or east to west?

An east–west orientation should give the maximum amount of sunlight to all parts of the polytunnel throughout the day. However, if tall crops are grown on the south side, shade can be a problem. Bear in mind that the sun doesn't always pass directly overhead: it traces a lower arc through the sky for a lot of the year.

If the structure runs north–south, take care when planting tall crops at the southern end.

Factor in the position of trees and structures that the sun will pass behind.

Can a polytunnel be put up on a slope?

The answer to this is yes, but you may need some expert help. If the slope runs along the length of the tunnel, there will be fewer complications than if it runs across the width. The site can of course be levelled first, or a small wall can be built for the lower edge of the polytunnel to sit on (foundation tubes can be concreted into this).

NOTE: Hoops should be vertical and preferably not at right angles to the slope.

What about electricity and water supplies?

A water supply is crucial and electricity is useful for a propagator, heater, etc. Try to site your polytunnel where it is easy to supply both of these services.

Is there enough space round the outer edges to allow room to work?

Allow a minimum of 1m/39in of access all around. This is essential for fixing the polythene in the first place, and also for replacing it as the years roll on. Washing the polythene down needs working space and so does getting from door to door around the outside (imagine if both doors need an extra weight propped against them in a strong wind). You will also need access to keep growth trimmed down around the tunnel – long grass and weeds can block light from low-growing plants.

A polytunnel can be put up on a sloping site

What sort of ground should the polytunnel go on?

You can always build up fertility by adding compost and manure, or you can grow plants in pots and growbags, so theoretically any sort of soil will do. On the other hand, if you have a well-dug soil that is rich in nutrients, go for that as a first choice. The polytunnel will be put under higher demands than any other part of the garden, so if it's an option, you might as well start out with the best that you've got.

NOTE: If there's a lot of rock on the site, positioning the foundation tubes can be difficult. There is scope to move the tubes a small bit, but the best thing is to go round with a straight crowbar first and make sure you can drive this into the ground at the relevant points.

Do polytunnels need planning permission?

This question often arises and the best answer is to contact the local planning authority and ask. It's sometimes easiest to visit the office in person in order to get a definitive ruling. Planning permission is not usually required for sheds and greenhouses (outbuildings), provided they conform to certain rules. Although polytunnels may not be specifically mentioned, they are usually considered to fit into the same category.

Different rules may apply if the polytunnel is to be erected on farmland, for agricultural use, or if it will be positioned more than 20m/66ft from a road or other dwelling.

Planning regulations change. For up-to-date information, check an authoritative website:
- Guidelines for England and Wales can be found at: www.planningportal.gov.uk (look in the section for outbuildings).
- Guidelines for Scotland can be obtained through local councils or planning authorities. See www.scotland.gov.uk for contact details.
- Guidelines for Northern Ireland can be found at: www.planningni.gov.uk.
- Guidelines for Ireland can be found at: www.irishstatutebook.ie (look under statutory instruments, planning and development regulations).

NOTE: 'Curtilage' means an area of land attached to a house and forming one enclosure within it.

England and Wales

Under new regulations that came into effect on 1 October 2008 outbuildings are considered to be permitted development, not needing planning permission, subject to the following limits and conditions:

- No outbuilding on land forward of a wall forming the principal elevation.
- Maximum eaves height of 2.5m and maximum overall height of 4m with a dual pitched roof, or 3m for any other roof.
- Maximum height of 2.5m if within 2m of a boundary of the curtilage of the dwelling house.
- No verandas, balconies or raised platforms.
- No more than half the area of land around the 'original house'* would be covered by additions or other buildings.

- In National Parks, the Broads, Areas of Outstanding Natural Beauty and World Heritage Sites the maximum area to be covered by buildings, enclosures, containers and pools more than 20m from house to be limited to 10 sq. m.
- On designated land* buildings, enclosures, containers and pools at the side of properties will require planning permission.
- Within the curtilage of listed buildings any outbuilding will require planning permission.

*The term 'original house' means the house as it was first built, or as it stood on 1 July 1948 (if it was built before that date). Although you may not have built an extension to the house, a previous owner may have done so.

*Designated land includes national parks and the Broads, Areas of Outstanding Natural Beauty, conservation areas and World Heritage Sites.

Source: www.planningportal.gov.uk

The above regulations are pretty much the same for **Northern Ireland** and **Scotland**. In Scotland, permission may be required if the structure is within 1m of a boundary. If in any doubt, ask the planning department of the county council.

Ireland

Exempted development relating to the construction, erection or placing within the curtilage of the house of any tent, awning, shade or other object, greenhouse, garage, store, shed or other similar structure:

1. No such structure shall be constructed, erected or placed forward of the front wall of a house.
2. The total area of such structures constructed, erected or placed within the curtilage of a house shall not, taken together with any other such structures previously constructed, erected or placed within the said curtilage, exceed 25 sq. m.
3. The construction, erection or placing within the curtilage of a house of any such structure shall not reduce the amount of private open space reserved exclusively for the use of the occupants of the house to the rear or to the side of the house to less than 25 sq. m.
4. The external finishes of any garage or other structure constructed, erected or placed to the side of a house, and the roof covering where any such structure has a tiled or slated roof, shall conform with those of the house.
5. The height of any such structure shall not exceed, in the case of a building with a tiled or slated pitched roof, 4m or, in any other case, 3m.
6. The structure shall not be used for human habitation or for the keeping of pigs, poultry, pigeons, ponies or horses, or for any other purpose other than a purpose incidental to the enjoyment of the house as such.

Source: www.irishstatutebook.ie

CHOOSING THE POLYTUNNEL

Do a search for polytunnels on the computer and you'll see that there is plenty of choice out there! Tunnels come in different shapes and sizes; they cost different amounts accordingly and most people want to get the best structure they can, for the best price.

Consider what shape you want – a hooped tunnel, a geodesic dome or a greenhouse-style pitched roof? Some hooped frames have straight sides, so more use can be made of the edges of beds inside. A lot of this is down to personal preference and the suitability of the site. A short, wide tunnel will fit some sites better than a long, narrow one.

Then there are issues like the strength of the structure, especially if the site is buffeted by strong winds. Some frames are made of stronger steel, and base rails or anchor plates can help give more stability. Horizontal bracing bars across each hoop are also good in windy conditions and they are ideal for hanging things off, or for fixing shelves to. And it is worth noting that if polythene is fitted to a base rail rather than being buried, it is easier to replace.

There is also the choice of cover. Some structures have the option of rolling the polythene up along the sides to provide extra ventilation; a mesh screen covers the

Bubble polythene gives extra strength for exposed sites (Keder)

opening sections. There's polythene that will last at least four years, or five years, or more. There is bubble polythene for extra insulation (this also performs well in exposed sites) and a milky-coloured one to reduce the effects of too much sun. Some polythene reduces the amount of condensation and hence reduces 'drip' when you are working inside.

Any extras cost more, but they can be well worth it. Don't rush the decision: take all the time that you need to make the right choice.

A roller simplifies side opening (Haygrove)

Important things to consider when buying

- Buy from a reputable supplier. Look at websites and ask around before making a choice.
- Choose a frame that is strong enough for the site.
- Get the strongest, longest-lasting polythene you can afford. Replacing polythene is a big job.
- Choose large enough doors to adequately ventilate the space.
- Look at strong doors and catches: buy them, or make them if you know how.
- Look at things like anti-fog polythene, which reduces the amount of condensation inside the polytunnel.
- Anti hot-spot tape is good around joints in the frame, which might snag or tear the polythene. Personally, I don't think it's worth putting it over the entire frame. I have a tunnel where polythene is still intact after sixteen years of direct contact with the galvanized hoops.
- Always buy a big fat roll of repair tape at the same time as buying the polytunnel.

Large polytunnels need effective ventilation (Keder)

PREPARING THE LAND

Digging the site

Covering with manure and polythene

To dig or not to dig?

Most people are in such a hurry to get the polytunnel up – and doing this can be constrained by weather – that preparation of the land is postponed. At its simplest, all long growth must be cut down to create a clear workspace; the tunnel is then erected on the cleared site. This is fine if the plan is to make raised beds, which are destined to be filled with imported material. It's also fine if the plan is to apply a thick mulch to the ground's surface and to leave this to rot down to help build a good growing medium. It isn't so fine if the plan is to dig, or mechanically cultivate, once the polytunnel is up.

If the plan is to use a **mechanical tiller or cultivator** on the plot, it's definitely best to do so before putting up the polytunnel. In any event, don't use it close to the polythene edge – there is no sense in damaging the polythene as soon as it is put on. If concrete base plates were used along the sides these will give some protection, but handles and levers can still cause damage higher up. A cultivator can be used up and down the middle of a large polytunnel, but it can be hard to manoeuvre a bulky machine inside a small space.

It's worth noting that simply chopping the soil can multiply weed problems unless this action is repeated several times over several weeks.

Deep digging is an ideal way to prepare the ground. You can incorporate manure or compost at the same time and dig weeds out. If the polytunnel has straight sides, it isn't impossible to do this once the structure is up. Just take care not to pierce the polythene, if this goes close to the ground on each side. If the tunnel has curved hoops, it can be hard to dig close to the edges. A short-handled fork or spade is essential and do take a stretch every now and then to ease the pressure on a bent back.

Best of all is to mark out the beds and dig these deeply before the tunnel goes up. Or, in order to avoid too much trampling by the construction crew, dig the beds once the hoops are in place, before the polythene cover is put on.

If time is short, laying a thick layer of compost or well-rotted manure directly on to the ground is a good option. This can be covered with a layer of black polythene or woven mulching material. Straw is also an option for mulch, but leave it outside for a few weeks to let any chemical sprays wash away if it isn't of the organic kind, as some chemicals can inhibit plant growth. A crop of potatoes under the mulch can be a good first-year plan. When these are dug, the soil will be left in good condition for any follow-on crops.

NOTE: It will save time for the erecting crew if trenches for burying polythene have been dug beforehand.

Check the acidity of the soil

A testing kit, or meter, won't cost very much and it will give valuable information about the pH (acidity/alkalinity) of the soil. Some plants do better on an acid soil and some prefer a more alkaline one. In general, aim for a pH of around 6.5 (just on the acid side of neutral), which will provide a suitable growing medium for most plants.

A reading of pH7 shows a neutral soil. Below this the soil gets more acid as the number decreases. A scattering of hydrated lime will bring the reading up closer to neutral. Ashes from burning wood are alkaline and if these are added to an acid soil they will also help to raise the pH.

If soil has a pH of greater than 7 it is considered alkaline. This can be harder to correct than an acid soil, but it isn't impossible and particularly so within the defined area of a polytunnel. Adding well-rotted manure can lower the pH, as can compost. Sulphur chips will also lower pH. They are slow acting and will work for two to three years if incorporated into the soil.

☑ A quick way to find out about the properties of your soil is to ask an enthusiastic gardening neighbour.

Testing the acidity of the soil

PUTTING UP A CLASSIC HOOPED POLYTUNNEL

A lot of people choose to employ someone to put the polytunnel up for them. The usual deal is that the site should be cleared and prepared beforehand. Ask the supplier if they have staff of their own who will put the tunnel up, or if they can recommend someone.

It's not hard to put up a polytunnel. If you have a few DIY skills and a few tools, it's perfectly possible to make a good job of it. It isn't a quick job (allow two days for a small tunnel, longer for a larger one), nor a job for one person (three is a minimum). It's also much nicer to do the job on a warm, calm day than on a cold, wet or windy one.

The most important thing is to read the instructions very carefully. If there are things you don't understand, it's completely acceptable to phone the manufacturer and ask them to explain. It's worth familiarizing yourself with all the parts, and where they go, before beginning any assembly.

NOTE: Some polytunnel suppliers (e.g. First Tunnels) provide a DVD showing assembly instructions.

1. Decide when to put the polytunnel up. Choose a couple of days when the forecast is for warm, calm weather. The polythene will fit more tightly if it's put on when warm and so can shrink as temperatures fall. Don't try to put polythene on in windy conditions, as it's likely to flap and snag off any sharp object.
2. Use strong posts and string to mark out the site. Make sure corners are square; the two diagonal measurements from corner to corner should be the same. [fig.1]
3. Level any lumps and dips that might cause problems around the marked-out edges.
4. Mark out where the foundation tubes will go. These should be at the four corners and at even (usually around 180cm/6ft) spacing along the two sides. You can adjust the spacing slightly if the tubes drive into the ground more easily, but make sure you repeat the same adjustment on the opposite side. (Foundation tubes can be concreted in for more stability, or if using a base rail system.) [fig.2] Foundation tubes can be positioned at each end for the door frame, if this is the method you are using; alternatively, holes can be dug for the posts of a wooden door frame.
5. Use a block of wood across the top of the foundation tubes so that they don't distort when hammered into the ground. About 45cm/18in of the tube should be buried. The tubes must be vertical (use a level) so that the hoops don't tilt at odd angles when they are fitted.

6. If there are any rough edges that might tear polythene, file these smooth before assembling.

7. Assemble all the hoops on the ground. If horizontal bars are to be fitted across the top of the hoops, do this at this stage. [fig.3]

8. Stand the hoops up and fit them into the foundation tubes. [fig.4]

9. Fit the ridge bar and side bracing bars. Make sure the hoops are vertical before tightening up any joints. The structure should start to feel pretty steady at this point. [fig.5]

10. Fix door frames. These will be fastened into the rest of the framework according to the manufacturer's instructions. [fig.6]

11. Apply anti-hot-spot tape (or be inventive and use something like old nylon tights) to cushion any joints that might have rough edges and cause the polythene to tear.

12. If burying polythene, dig a trench 20cm/8in wide and 20cm/8in deep all around the edge except for across the door openings. This might have been done already, in which case skip on to the next step.

13. Unroll the plastic along one side of the frame. Make sure there are no sharp objects on the ground to puncture it. Lift the cover (into any breeze) so that it slides over the tunnel.

14. If possible, stand a person at each corner of the tunnel to hold the plastic down. A fifth person can go along putting a few shovels of soil into the trenches. The plastic should be as tight as possible.

NOTE: Tighten it with soft-shod feet rather than pulling and applying pressure points over fingernails. (If you are using a base-rail system the polythene will not be buried but will clip in place, leaving a flap on the ground on each side.) [fig.7]

15. Once the sides are provisionally weighted, each end of the polythene can be cut to fit the doors. The simplest way to avoid bagginess is to cut a V-shaped flap below the central point of the doorway and to roll the flap around a piece of timber. Pulling on the timber, at each end of the polytunnel, will stretch the polythene along its length.

16. Keep stretching the polythene and filling the trenches (or use the rail system) to get the polythene as tight as possible.

17. Fit the end pieces of polythene around the sides of the door frame. This might involve nailing battens to a wooden frame, or using clips on a metal frame. Try to get the ends of the tunnel as neat as possible, with any folds running downwards so that condensation doesn't collect.

18. Fit all doors and catches on the same day. [fig. 8]

LAYING OUT THE INSIDE OF THE POLYTUNNEL

There are several options as to the ground plan and you should consider all these before making any definite decisions. Get out a pen and paper and make a few sketches to help in the decision-making process.

NOTE: It helps if paths are wide enough to push a wheelbarrow along.

Option 1: A single central path with a bed on each side. This gives the maximum amount of border to use for growing, but it might mean treading on the soil in order to reach all parts. This is the most appropriate plan for a small tunnel.

Option 2: Two paths running the length of the polytunnel, which effectively divide the floor plan into three long beds. This gives easy access to all parts of the tunnel, possibly without having to tread on the beds. This is a good plan for a wide tunnel.

Option 3: Individual raised beds, with paths running in between. This gives easy access to all beds; they need never be trodden on and they can be raised to a height that makes work easier for gardeners with back problems. It means that less ground is available for cultivation and the height of the beds might be an issue, in that they reduce the 'head height' available for tall crops. This is a good plan for a very large tunnel where maximizing space is less of an issue.

LEFT:
A single path
RIGHT:
Raised beds

NOTE: Raised beds can be bought pre-made, or you can make your own. Never make them so big that you can't access all points by reaching in from the edge, or so deep that they hit against the polythene sides.

Option 4: Let your creativity take you where you want to go. Some people have decking, some have hot tubs and some have deckchairs to enjoy the space inside the polytunnel!

Making paths

Some people choose to make a permanent path, using paving stones or tiles. Others simply leave a dry dirt path. The choice is yours and things can evolve over the years. It does make a certain amount of sense to dig out pathways and add the soil on to the beds at each side.

Before laying tiles dig down to a firm base and level this with sand if necessary. Boards can be fitted at each side of the path. Nail these on to posts knocked into the ground. Boards will act as retaining walls, to stop earth falling back on to the paths, and they will help keep the beds raised when compost, etc., is added over the years.

A water supply

If water can be piped to a tap by the polytunnel door, this is ideal. A tap on the inside of the structure means that you don't have to keep running outside in bad weather to fill watering cans, and fittings are less likely to freeze in the winter. On the other hand, you can use hosepipes and watering systems to bring water from an outdoor tap.

Watering is a major job in a polytunnel and anything that helps with this is of course a bonus. There are lots of watering systems available, from the humble watering can to electronically controlled sprinkling devices, and I'm sure there are devotees to all forms. What follows are a few personal observations. The choice, as always, is with each individual polytunnel grower.

Overhead watering systems and sprinklers wouldn't be my favourite for a polytunnel. The environment is already heading towards too damp

A large polytunnel with a dirt path

A hosepipe delivers water right where it is needed

for some plants, which fare much better if leaves are kept dry. Some of these systems offer the greatest degree of control, however, and they may be best suited to very large polytunnels, or those where a limited range of crops grow.

Pipes that drip or weep water at ground level do a good job, with two provisos: one is that a good pressure of water is needed to make them work well (usually no problem with a mains water supply); the other is that pipes have to be laid in an evenly spaced pattern to ensure equal watering for all plants. It would take a lot of pipe to water the whole of a large tunnel in this way, but selective use of this system can benefit thirsty plants like tomatoes.

A hand-held hosepipe and spray nozzle will mean hours spent spraying water around the tunnel, but it will also mean getting exactly the right amount of water to exactly the right points. Leaves can be dampened if necessary, or they can be kept dry while the soil is soaked.

Water reservoirs made from cut-down bottles can make hand-watering easier. Reservoirs can be filled with a jet of water rather than having to sprinkle water slowly over the surface of the soil (a jet of water on to the soil can disturb plant roots). They cost nothing to make if you simply save milk and pop bottles: cut the bottoms off, remove the lids and put them spout end down into the ground.

The good old watering can might seem the worst method of all, but it has its advantages. If water is in short supply, watering with a can will ensure that every drop goes to a place where it is needed. Liquid feeds can be mixed with the water, so two jobs will be accomplished at the same time.

Water barrels and rain butts are vital where water supplies are low. These will collect water off any pitched roof, if gutters and downpipes are there to channel the supply. Some polytunnels can be fitted with gutters to do the same job. Wherever you put the barrels, try to choose a point close to the polytunnel, so that you don't have to walk miles to fill a watering can. Alternatively, if you elevate the container, it might be possible to create a gravity feed to pipe the water down to where it is needed.

Don't let water stand too long without using it. The idea is to have a good, fresh, clean water supply.

TOP: Pipes that drip water on to the soil
BOTTOM: Home-made water reservoir

☑ Put barrels of water inside the polytunnel to help raise temperatures through the winter months (see November).

Electricity
An electricity supply can be essential if you want to operate propagators, soil warming cables, lights, etc. However, the combination of electric sockets and a damp environment isn't ideal. Consult a qualified electrician, or install an outdoor power kit, which has armoured cable and connectors suitable for using outdoors (available from Two Wests & Elliott, for instance – see list of suppliers on page 195).

It isn't wise to use an ordinary extension lead inside a polytunnel.

Benches and shelves
A good potting bench isn't essential, but it is a useful thing to have. It doesn't need to be too big; nor does it need to be fixed to the structure. Freestanding units are available from many greenhouse suppliers. Choose one that is easy to scrub down and isn't too heavy to lift if you want to move it.

If you fancy a bit of DIY, it isn't too hard to make a bench. Just make sure that no nails or rough bits of timber are in a position to damage the polythene.

If your tunnel has horizontal bars running between the hoops, it's easy to hang shelves from these. It's easier still to rest a plank between the horizontal bars on two sets of hoops – although this might set the shelf too high.

Shelves can be fixed to the framework of a polytunnel. Use jubilee clips and hooks to get a fixing against the frame; these will ensure that the shelf doesn't slip. A wooden shelf can be suspended with a length of rope, but watch out for it swinging if it gets a knock.

NOTE: It's a good idea to protect the point between jubilee clip and polythene with a piece of hot-spot tape.

TOP: A good potting bench
MIDDLE: Fixing a jubilee clip and hook
BOTTOM: Hanging shelf

2
A FEW ESSENTIALS

A LIST OF USEFUL THINGS

A polytunnel is really just an empty shell. It contains a space that has the potential to be where fabulous food grows through the years ahead. All it takes is an enthusiastic gardener to set the process going and, before you know it, there will be tomatoes, peppers, strawberries and a host of other fruit and vegetables. The desire to start growing can be almost overwhelming, but any gardener needs a few tools to help grow the best crops.

The list below gives an idea of some basic tools and equipment. It may not be necessary to buy them all – some might already be part of your gardening stock; some can be borrowed and some can be made. You might not need propagation equipment in the first year of growing, if you buy in plants rather than raising them from seed. There again, some gardeners might already be able to tick every item on the list. The simplest thing is to read through the list and decide what is essential for you and what is not.

TOP:
Plenty of pots
BOTTOM:
Home-made labels

- A notebook and pen, to keep a record of the polytunnel year
- A fork, a spade, a hoe and a rake
- A trowel and hand fork might be useful too
- A pair of gardening gloves – especially if nettles are a common weed
- A bucket or two
- A watering can – essential even if you use other watering systems (see Part 1).
- A hosepipe, to bring water right to the point where it is needed
- A maximum and minimum thermometer – otherwise you will never know the highs and lows. A digital thermometer with remote sensors is a good idea: this makes it easy to spot when doors need to be opened or closed
- A range of pots, root-trainers and trays – from small cells to large containers. These can also be made from recycled fruit tubs, yoghurt pots, buckets, etc.
- Labels and a pencil or waterproof pen, so that you will always know the identity of each plant. Labels can be made from plastic milk bottles cut into strips
- Good-quality, organic compost suitable for seeds and for larger plants
- Growbags filled with organic compost

TOP: Wooden trays for holding pots
BOTTOM: Plastic bottles as mini cloches
RIGHT: Propagator

- Packets of seed – chosen with care from a good supplier
- A waterproof, airtight box for storing packets of seed
- A ball of strong string
- Canes for supporting tall plants
- Short sticks for marking each end of a row
- Plastic or wooden trays to hold several plants in pots – orange boxes will do, or make your own
- A bottle of organic liquid seaweed to use as a feed (for how to make your own liquid feeds, see Part 7)
- A pack of 'organic' slug pellets – ones based on ferric phosphate work well and are harmless to humans, pets and wildlife (other than slugs and snails)
- Horticultural fleece to cover plants on cold nights. Bags, old sheets, newspaper, cardboard boxes, etc. will also do the job
- Bubble polythene and clear plastic bags, to cover pots of germinating seeds
- A cloche or small cold frame, to give extra protection when raising tender plants in the polytunnel early in the year
- A heated propagator – a heat mat, or soil-warming cables, and a cloche to go over the top
- Unheated mini propagators – essentially trays or cells with plastic lids
- A pH meter, or kit, for testing soil acidity
- Secateurs
- A soil thermometer, to show when the soil is warm enough to sow in or plant things out
- A roll of aluminium foil to reflect more light on sun-loving plants
- Plastic bottles to act as mini cloches

SOME THOUGHTS ON SEEDS

Buying seeds

It's worth spending an hour or two browsing through seed catalogues (see the list of suppliers on page 195). This is an easy way to consider the pros and cons of different varieties and make choices at your leisure. If you are organized, you can put the whole year's order together in one go. Write out a wish list, price it up and then delete any excessive choices if it runs over budget. For the greatest ease, place an order online and have it delivered to your door – allowing enough time, as seeds can take two or three weeks to arrive. Alternatively, find out which brands of seed your local garden centre stocks and get hold of appropriate catalogues in advance. This enables you to shop with a prepared list, so that you don't have to stand for hours reading packets in the shop. Always have alternative options in case some varieties aren't available.

☑ Ordering in the winter means you are more likely to get popular varieties before they sell out. It will also help you to organize the planting plan for the year ahead. Of course, you might also have some seed saved from the year before.

Packets of old seed

Get out the pile of old seed packets from that biscuit tin! Check through and see what seeds are still viable and which should have been thrown out at the end of the last growing season. Some seed is fine for several years, but other seed is only really viable

Plenty of choice when ordering seeds

Peas for planting

for one year. It's a good idea to write down how much seed is left, and what date it should be sown by, on the front of each packet. This saves hunting for the tiny print on the back.

It can still be worth trying to germinate seed from a packet that is past its 'best before' date. Some may work, but don't rely on it, especially if the seed has a long germination time. New seed will grow faster, with more seeds germinating every time.

Some tips on organizing packets of seed

• Seed keeps best in a cool, dark, dry environment. The house is probably too warm and the polytunnel is certainly too damp (before you even begin to consider the temperature swings). A shed, a cool bedroom or the fridge might be the best place.

• An old shoebox is a good container for lining up packets in, if the cool and dry elements can be ensured. Otherwise, find a sealable plastic box and add a pack of silica gel to keep seed dry at all times.

• It's a good idea to use pieces of card to divide up the months and to sort packets by sowing time. If something like lettuce is to be used for repeat sowings, simply move the packet into the next month's section after you have made all the sowings in the current month. There will be lots of packets in the February, March and April sections and fewer in January, but there are always some seeds that can be sown. If there are no packets in the sections from July onwards, get out the catalogues again and think about what seed you need for autumn and winter crops.

Is seed still viable?

Most seed packets state what date the contents should be used by, but once the foil packs are opened seed viability starts to decline. A few specifics:

• As a general rule, I buy aubergine, melon, sweetcorn and pepper seed fresh each year. If you have seed left over from last year, some of it will probably germinate, but by the time you find out that only two out of the ten sweetcorn seeds have made it, you will have lost a lot of growing time.

• Tomato seed is good for two years.

• Cucumbers and courgettes will germinate well in a second year and even in a third.

• All brassicas have long lives and seed will be fine after three or four years. Even five-year-old cabbage seed can germinate well, but, as with all seed, it must be kept cool and dry.

• Spinach, Swiss chard and beetroot all give good germination for up to three years.

• Lettuce will give reduced germination in year two, but if you sow thickly there should still be plenty of plants.

• Carrots, beans and peas aren't worth saving for a second year. Buy just enough for one year at a time.

SOME THOUGHTS ON COMPOST

Buying in compost or making your own?

A bag of compost doesn't really go that far if you intend growing lots of different plants. If the supplier is likely to run out, buy at least three or four bags. I would always advocate using good organic compost. This will have plenty of nutrients to feed growing plants for six to eight weeks. After that point, plants can be given a liquid feed, or moved into larger pots, or planted out.

For a cheaper option, you can make your own compost mixes (see Part 7), but do sieve these to remove large lumps, worms, etc. Home-made compost is perfect for potting on larger plants.

Which type of compost for which type of plant?

Some bought compost contains large chunks of material. This is fine for larger plants but can be hopeless for seedlings. Break up what you can with your fingers and evict large solid pieces, or pass the lot through a riddle if necessary. Seedlings do best in a fine crumbly mix.

If compost holds too much water, this can lead to difficulties with seedlings damping off. Heavily peat-based composts suffer in this way (they are also not very environmentally friendly, unless they use reclaimed peat). On the other hand, coarse compost can drain too quickly and be prone to drying out. It's often a question of trial and error, but I would suggest:

- Moisture-retaining compost for resilient plants that need plenty of water like tomatoes, courgettes, beans and peas.
- Free-draining compost for raising more delicate plants like basil, cucumbers, peppers, melons and sweetcorn.

Use a moisture-retaining compost for tomatoes

3

A MONTH-BY-MONTH GUIDE TO A YEAR IN THE POLYTUNNEL

JANUARY

January brings a moment of calm, with Christmas a thing of the past and some New Year gardening resolutions firmly in place. The months to come will get busier and busier, so use this one well to ensure that everything is organized for the year ahead.

If the polytunnel is empty now, it's worth trying a few early sowings. It will be several weeks before any of these are big enough to harvest, but the sight of seeds freshly sown in compost is the first exciting hint of the bountiful crops to come.

Weather report

January can bring some of the coldest weather of the year and some of the hardest frosts. Temperatures below 0°C/32°F are common enough and there is a strong possibility of snow in all but a few milder coastal extremes.

January jobs in brief

Keep a diary, make a plan and order seeds
Make a few early sowings if weather permits
Sow aubergines in pots at 20°C/68°F
Plant out lettuce sown last November
Plant out mangetout peas and broad beans sown
    last autumn
Keep light levels as high as possible
Keep on top of repairs to the polythene
Water sparingly and only if necessary
Start feeding crops
Bring strawberry pots in from the cold
Finish pruning grape vines

Sowing
mangetout peas

Try sowing in January

A few early carrots
Mangetout peas
Salad leaves – rocket, mizuna, mibuna
Spring lettuce varieties
Radishes

Making plans

Spades and hoes may be obvious tools for the garden, but don't forget the notebook and pen: keep a diary of the polytunnel year as it unfolds and this will be an invaluable tool in the years ahead. Make a note of when you sow seeds and how well they germinate, when crops are ready to eat, what things do well and what fails. If there are problems with particular pests and diseases, write these down as well, and always date each entry. The more information, the merrier – or at least, the more use the notebook will be next year, when the process starts all over again.

OPPOSITE:
January
polytunnel

It's a good idea to dedicate the first page to a wish list of all that you would like to grow in the polytunnel. On the next page, draw a sketch plan showing how all these crops will fit in – or not, in which case you may have to cross some things off the list.

If possible, the plan of the tunnel should be divided into four quarters, so that you can practise crop rotation on a four-year cycle (see Part 6). A crop like tomatoes may occupy one of the quarters, in which case this crop will not be grown in the same spot for another four years. In a small polytunnel, tomatoes may take up half of the space, but these can at least be moved to the opposite side every other year.

☑ Tomatoes, peppers and aubergines grow better in a drier atmosphere, whereas cucumbers, courgettes and melons prefer a humid one. It isn't really possible to provide both sets of ideal conditions at once, but when drawing up a planting plan try to group accordingly.

Is it too early to sow seeds?
There are three things to consider before making any sowings in an unheated polytunnel in January:
- What temperature do the seeds need to germinate?
- How warm is the soil inside the polytunnel?
- Might this be an anomaly, or is the temperature likely to stay roughly the same at this time of the year, in this part of the country?

Of course, it can be hard to predict what the weather will do for more than a few days, and the possibilities can vary wildly from year to year. However, it is usually possible to make some educated guesses based on local knowledge. In southern parts of the UK and Ireland it is often possible to make a few sowings in mid-January. In the Midlands it may be best to wait until the end of the month and in the north of Scotland buy a propagator, or wait a few weeks more before sowing without heat.

Having said that, there is little to lose by trying a few early sowings and the gains can be great in a mild year. A polytunnel really does make a difference: it's amazing to watch seedlings push through in weather that seems too cold to allow anything to grow. If the first sowings don't work, try again next month, but don't leave it too late for a shot at the earliest crops. Wait until a cold snap is over and choose the right moment. So long as seed germinates and seedlings push through, it doesn't much matter if growth is then slowed by another cold spell.

Covering trays with bubble wrap

☑ Soil in the polytunnel will usually be a degree or two warmer than that outside. To make it warmer still, and to protect seeds in trays, use cloches, bubble wrap or fleece to hold in the heat.

Carrots
If the polytunnel is large enough, you can sow carrots directly into the border. It isn't worth having later varieties taking up space, but the earliest ones will give tasty young roots several weeks ahead of ones grown outdoors. 'Early Nantes' and

'Amsterdam Forcing' perform particularly well from late January sowings, but if the winter is cold wait until February.

Possibly the best way to get a crop of sweet young roots is to sow seed thickly in a 30cm/12in pot. Just cover the seed with compost, water lightly and cover the pot with a triple layer of fleece until seedlings emerge. Not all seed will germinate, and not all seedlings will survive, but a good scattering of slim leaves should start to appear in two to three weeks' time.

☑ To repel slugs, raise the pot on a brick or stones, raised above a moat of water. These pests adore young carrot seedlings and can munch through an entire pot as soon as shoots appear.

Planting early potatoes

Potatoes in the border

Some people like to grow a crop of early potatoes in the border soil. Allow 30cm/12in between plants and the same between rows. If plants are protected from frost, and if they are well fed and watered, a January sowing can give a good return of tasty spuds in late April or May – much earlier than ones sown outdoors. However, if temperatures are consistently lower than 5°C/41°F, leave potatoes to chit in the shed and wait until February before planting them out in the polytunnel.

A potato crop will break up new soil and create a more friable, workable structure for later crops, but there are a couple of drawbacks:

- The potatoes may not be ready to harvest before the space is needed for more valuable crops such as cucumbers and tomatoes.
- If the potatoes become infected with blight, this disease can spread from the potato leaves to the more valuable tomato crop growing near by.

☑ Try mulching around potatoes with black polythene or straw. This warms the soil and suppresses weeds. You will raise a faster crop this way, but watch out for slugs hiding underneath the mulch.

Mulching with straw

Potatoes in containers

In an average-sized polytunnel, there probably isn't enough space to grow potatoes in the border. The best solution is to grow some in buckets or large containers. These can be moved outdoors, if necessary, as the weather improves. Put a 5cm/2in-deep layer of compost in the bottom of a bucket. Choose an early variety, like 'Orla', and put one or two chitted seed potatoes (ones with green shoots just emerging from the tuber) on top of the layer of compost. There should be some holes in the bottom of the container to allow good drainage. A bucket with a split across the bottom will drain well enough; otherwise use a drill, or melt holes with a hot nail. Take care: steel conducts heat! Use pliers to hold the nail and be careful not to burn anyone in the process.

Mizuna and mibuna

Cover the seed potatoes with a further 5cm/2in of compost and cover with bubble polythene or fleece if nights are cold. Young shoots will take a few weeks to appear.

Mizuna, mibuna and rocket

These tasty salad leaves do extremely well from a January sowing. Sow directly into drills filled with compost, marking the rows with sticks and string. Use a good pinch of seed for every 25cm/10in of row. Remember that seed can be slower to germinate when the soil is cold and more seed will fail now than in a couple of months' time. Cover the seed with a 5mm layer of soil.

NOTE: Slugs and snails will eat emerging mizuna seedlings in preference to mibuna or rocket. The latter two have a spicier flavour, which may not suit a mollusc's taste. Once mizuna plants are a few centimetres tall, slugs seem to leave them alone.

Lettuce

Choose looseleaf, butterhead or cos varieties to sow at this time of year. These are reasonably hardy and do surprisingly well from an early sowing. It may be cold when you sow the seed, but the days are lengthening and soil in a polytunnel soon starts to warm up.

Choose two or three varieties to give a greater chance of success. 'Salad Bowl' is a good early looseleaf variety that deserves its popularity. It is a good performer for the beginner or experienced gardener, although the green variety usually does better than the red from such an early sowing. 'Little Gem' is a favourite cos type that is quick to mature and gives crunchy leaves in late April or May. Choose 'All the Year Round' for a butterhead lettuce from such an early start. These are reliable performers in an average year. Try sowing other favourite varieties, as they may work equally well, but leave sowings of crisphead and iceberg varieties until February or March.

> ☑ Such early sowings of lettuce do best if seedlings are raised in trays or pots and planted out to their final growing position when 4cm/1½in tall. This method avoids gaps in rows and makes it easier to provide extra protection on cold nights. It also allows you to select the strongest seedlings for planting out and, in a mild winter, it is easier to keep young plants away from the ravages of slugs and snails.

Sowing lettuce

Sowing lettuce

Sow seed thinly in pots or tubs, and just cover with a scattering of compost. Water lightly so that the compost is damp, but not soggy, and cover with a layer of bubble polythene. If the temperature in the polytunnel falls below 5°C/41°F, cover with a clear plastic tub or cloche, to retain some extra warmth. You can use a propagator, but set it no higher than 10°C/50°F. Or you can start seeds on a window ledge in the house, but don't leave them there too long: if you do, the seedlings will grow leggy and weak. The aim is to produce strong, hardy plants. Germination takes six to ten days. It can be slower if it is really cold. Remove the bubble polythene once seedlings are up, and the cloche once temperatures rise above 10°C/50°F.

Tender plants

It can be tempting to sow **tomatoes, peppers, melons, cucumbers,** etc., in January and this would indeed give plants an early start. However, young plants will soon outgrow the propagator or window ledge – and they can do this several weeks before the polytunnel is warm enough for you to plant them out. The earliest that some of these crops can be planted out is late April or early May. In a cold year, or a cold part of the country, planting might have to wait until late May, or even early June. If you put a heater in the polytunnel for a few weeks in March, April and May, or if you use a very large propagator, by all means sow early, but nothing will be lost by waiting until February or early March to get most tender crops under way.

☑ There are exceptions to any rule and aubergines are the one tender plant I would sow in January.

Aubergines

Some people find aubergines easy to grow and some find them difficult. An early start is one of the tricks of getting good fruit. These plants usually crop best in a rich, fertile growing medium. Ideally, temperatures shouldn't fall below 15°C/59°F and there should be plenty of sun while the fruit swells.

Sowing an early variety such as 'Moneymaker' or 'Black Enorma' in January allows plants to flower early enough in the summer to give the best chance of fruit. Plants will have to be nurtured through a few cold months. If this seems like too much work, buy young plants instead in a few weeks' time.

Sow seed in a pot of compost in the last week of January (or first week of February if that's how it works out). Sprinkle compost over the top to a depth of 6mm. Few people need more than three or four aubergine plants, so sow twice that many and choose the best to grow on. The compost should be damp, but not wet. Place the pot inside a plastic bag and use a rubber band to hold the bag in place. Aim to keep the pot at a temperature of 20–25°C/68–77°F, but in practice a warm window ledge will do the job, even if temperatures fluctuate a little outside this range. Germination can take 7–21 days.

Winter lettuce

Plant out some sowings from last year

If your enthusiasm for polytunnel growing didn't wane towards the end of the previous year, you should have young plants in pots all ready to go into their permanent home.

Winter lettuce planted out now will be ready to eat in a few weeks' time. Whether it goes into a growbag, a larger pot or the border soil, any young plant will appreciate the move; roots should never be left to grow until restricted and deprived of nutrients, for leaves will yellow and plants will bolt while small.

Kohl rabi

Use a table fork to ease young plants out of the pot with as much of the root ball as possible. For winter lettuce, allow 20cm/8in between plants and the same between rows; these do not grow quite as large as their summer counterparts. Water lightly but don't soak the soil.

Kohl rabi can be planted 20cm/8in apart in rows 25cm/10in apart. This is slightly closer than it says on the packets, but it works fine for producing tennis-ball-sized tasty roots.

> ☑ Before planting out small plants, fill drills with a mix of two parts well-rotted compost to one part leafmould. This will not only feed them but also keep the roots in a moist growing medium.

Mangetout peas

If you sowed seed in pots last autumn, you may well have planted out seedlings in December. If not, the young plants will now be around 10cm/4in tall and starting to flop in the pots. These should go into the ground as soon as possible.

Dig a trench to one spade's depth and half fill this with compost from the garden heap. It doesn't matter if the compost is fairly coarse – it will continue to rot in the trench and will hold a good supply of water. Peas and beans can make their own nitrogen, but they need this layer of moisture-retaining material to keep them supplied throughout the thirsty times ahead.

Fill the top of the trench with loose soil and plant the peas into this. Try to tip the whole root ball out of the pot. If the seed was multiple-sown in tubs, the root ball should come out intact and the peas should be at an appropriate spacing. It is possible to move individual plants a little – aim for a double row 12cm/5in apart with roughly 5cm/2in between plants. Make a depression in the soil to fit plants and roots at the same level, or just slightly deeper than they were in the pot. Firm gently with both hands so that the young plants aren't loose in the soil. No seeds or roots should be visible.

Planting mangetout peas

> ☑ If you didn't sow mangetout peas last autumn it is still worth making a January sowing in the polytunnel. 'Oregon Sugar Pod' is a good variety, as it withstands low temperatures. Either sow in tubs, or seed can go directly into the ground at this time of year. If sowing direct, make a double row with 12cm/5in between the two rows and 5cm/2in between peas in each row. Cover with 5cm/2in soil.

☑ Peas and beans prefer a neutral to alkaline soil. If the soil is acid (you can buy a kit to test for this), scatter a little hydrated lime, or wood ash, along the row.

Broad beans

If you sowed a winter-hardy variety of broad bean, such as 'Aquadulce Claudia', in pots in November or December, young plants will be ready for planting out in January. Make sure you choose a spot close to a door, in order to get the best set of early flowers; broad beans will self-pollinate, but pollination is more successful if bees can have easy access to the flowers. Make a trench and plant out as for peas (above), allowing 20cm/8in between the double row and 15cm/6in between plants.

NOTE: There is no advantage to sowing broad bean seed in January for a polytunnel crop. Plants take up space and will not crop at a significantly different time to ones sown under a cloche outdoors. However, it might be worth sowing one or two seeds in pots to fill any gaps in outdoor rows.

Strawberries

Strawberries grow really well in a polytunnel and can produce extra-early crops. Young plants in pots should have been out of the tunnel since last summer. They need a touch of frost to help them flower well, but by January they should have had this and they will be ready to bring back under cover. Give all plants a health check before bringing them into the tunnel. Remove discoloured leaves and check the root ball of failing plants to see if any vine weevil grubs are in residence. If so, squash each and every grub before repotting all plants in fresh compost.

Removing discoloured leaves from strawberry plants

Lay a thick layer of manure on top of the border soil and put the pots in a row on top of this. If you use fresh manure it will help heat the pots as it rots. Roots take several weeks to grow out of the pot and into the manure, by which time it will have broken down enough to cause no harm. If the timing is right, the manure provides a good nutrient boost just when the fruit is swelling. Plants brought indoors at the beginning of January should ripen fruit in early May.

☑ Keep pots pretty dry for a couple of weeks until new growth starts.

Grape vines

If you didn't prune and tidy the vine at the end of last year, do the job now before it starts into new growth. Vines fruit on new growth, so prune back shoots from the previous year to leave one fat bud. It's always worth checking and removing any dieback after a period of temperatures below 0°C/32°F – there may be some dead wood that you missed last year.

Frozen veg!

Plant growth stops at temperatures below 5°C/41°F and if it is cold enough, for long enough, plants can freeze inside a polytunnel. If this happens, fill a watering can with

Removing snow

cool (not freezing or warm) water and pour this over any affected foliage. The idea is to melt any ice before the sun hits. Plants may look a bit sorry for themselves for a few days, but many will make a full recovery.

Of course, if a really cold spell is forecast it's best to cover plants with an extra insulating layer.

Light levels

Days are short at this time of year and the amount of light getting through to growing plants can be limited. A small fall of snow is no problem, even if it covers the tunnel: it will often slip free and slide down the polythene. If snow covers the structure for more than one day, however, or if it builds up to a weight that may cause old polythene to split, it is a problem. Use a soft, long-handled brush to sweep snow away. Alternatively, use the brush to lift the polythene from the inside and the snow should slide off. Use the latter technique only if polythene is sound.

The winter months are a good time to remove any branches and prune back any hedges that shade the polytunnel. This is always much harder after a spurt of spring growth, or when trees and shrubs are full of leaf. Take care not to damage polythene with falling branches, especially if these have spines or thorns. Larger branches may need the attention of a tree surgeon – always call in a professional if in doubt.

Repair any rips

Look after the polythene cover of the tunnel. With care, this can last ten years and twenty isn't unknown. Replacing the cover is an expensive and time-consuming job, but regular checks and repairs can defer the date when it needs to be replaced (for how to repair polythene, see Part 6).

Time for a liquid feed

As overwintered plants start into new growth, they need an extra bit of feed to push them along. Don't rely on the leftover nutrients in a tired bed. Start using the liquid manures you made at the end of last year, or mix up a new batch early in January for use at the end of the month (for making liquid feeds, see Part 7). It's amazing how late-winter crops can get moving over the next few weeks.

☑ Wait until soil temperatures are above 5°C/41°F before applying a liquid feed.

Enjoy the January harvest

Spinach
Swiss chard
Pak choi
Kohl rabi
Florence fennel
Spring cabbage
Beetroot
Turnip
Broccoli
Kale
Parsley
Lettuce
Oriental and salad leaves

Swiss chard
'Bright Lights'

Some harvesting hints

- If temperatures are below 0°C/32°F for a long period, some of the less hardy crops, such as **Florence fennel,** may not survive. Cover with several layers of fleece to give them the best chance until temperatures rise. Eat fennel while young and juicy. If using the foliage, take a little from each plant.
- If the large outer leaves of crops such as **spinach, Swiss chard** and **beetroot** are covered with grey spots that have reddish edges, remove affected leaves. These are unsightly and tough and are best not eaten. New leaves will grow to replace them.
- Keep picking cut-and-come-again crops even if leaves are small.
- Never strip a plant completely, or take out the growing point.
- Take outer leaves off **lettuce** if you don't need the whole plant. More will grow at the centre.
- Be patient with **sprouting broccoli:** don't nip out the first central spike until it bulks out and a few side shoots grow.

Cut-and-come-again crops

FEBRUARY

February can come creeping up, pretending that it's still part of winter and the garden should be asleep. Don't be fooled! Of course February can produce some cold, nasty weather, but a polytunnel can be a few weeks ahead of the great outdoors. There is heat in the sun, things are starting to warm up and the days are lengthening enough to stimulate plant growth. It's time to start sowing for summer crops.

Weather report

February can be a bitterly cold month with easterly winds bringing snow and frosts that linger right through the day. On the other hand, the month can bring sunshine as well and temperatures in a polytunnel will be on the rise: 25°C/77°F is perfectly possible on a sunny day, even if the wind is blowing outside. Soil temperatures also increase in the polytunnel, but don't be complacent – February can bring air temperatures so low that plants under cover start to freeze.

February jobs in brief

Wash the polythene and frame
Scrub down fixtures and fittings
Set up a propagator or clear a
    window ledge
Sow tomatoes and peppers
Make sowings for early outdoor crops

Provide support for peas
Catch up on jobs that should have been
    done by now
Warm the soil
Start collecting tomato poles, compost, etc.
Keep harvesting

Setting up a propagator

Time to sow

Tomatoes
Peppers
Aubergines – if not sown last month
Melons – provided they can be kept warm
Early carrots and potatoes
Lettuce
Spinach
Salad leaves
Kohl rabi
Beetroot, leeks and celeriac – for an early
   start to outdoor crops

Keep harvesting

Raising tender plants from seed

Plants such as tomatoes, peppers and melons benefit from a long growing season. If you start seed off at the end of February, plants will be large and strong enough to take full advantage of a hot May and June. This early advantage can see them cropping well even in a poor July and August.

Seeds can be germinated in an airing cupboard, on a warm window ledge, or in a propagator. Choose a place where the temperature is fairly constant and doesn't rise above 25°C/77°F or fall below 15°C/59°F.

Light is often an aid to good germination and, of course, this is essential once the seedlings poke through. If light is limited, seedlings will grow 'leggy' and pale.

☑ For years, I shuffled pots between sunny window ledges and airing cupboards, making the trek with young plants to the polytunnel on warm days and back into the heat of the house at night. It can be done, and wonderful healthy plants can be grown this way. But it is a lot of work and there are much simpler solutions. Heating the polytunnel is one answer, but this is expensive. Heating a small area within the polytunnel is a much better plan. Small propagators don't cost a lot. They are good for germinating seed and raising small plants. If you plan to grow larger plants from seed, buy a large propagator (or a heat mat and make a large cloche cover yourself). This will be home to several small plants for two or three months.

Get sowing

Use a good potting compost and preferably an organic one. Think how many plants you need and sow just a *few* extra seeds. It's better to grow the right number of healthy plants than to waste time, effort and valuable space on surplus plants. Follow instructions on packets of seed. Some seeds do best uncovered and some like to be hidden beneath a layer of compost.

After sowing, water lightly and evenly, so that the compost is damp but not soggy – better too dry than too wet. Put trays and pots into plastic bags, or cover with a layer of clear polythene if the tray is too large to fit into a bag. Seeds that take seven days to germinate shouldn't need watering again until seedlings appear. Seeds that take longer to germinate should be checked once or twice, so that the compost doesn't dry out.

Label each pot

☑ Label each pot and tray clearly so that you know exactly what is growing where. Use waterproof plant labels and a pencil, or indelible ink, so that the details don't wash away or fade. Lots of seedlings look the same – even if you think you will remember what everything is, you probably won't in a few weeks' time.

Tomatoes

Sow seed in late February to give the best chance of ripe fruit at the end of June. March and April sowings will also give good crops, but they won't produce ripe fruit until July or August. Sow seed in trays or pots – one per variety – and just cover with a sprinkling of compost. Put in a plastic bag and keep at 20°C/68°F if possible. Seedlings will pop up in six to ten days. Don't leave them unchecked in an airing cupboard.

Tomatoes come in many sizes

Tomato varieties

Cherry varieties produce the earliest crops. Sow at least one variety of these; if there are children in the family, two or three varieties will always get eaten. 'Sungold', 'Sakura' and 'Gardener's Delight' are great varieties, but everyone has their own favourites.

Medium-sized tomatoes seem to crop abundantly. These can be used fresh, but they are also good for bottling and freezing. 'Shirley' is an old favourite that produces reliable crops. 'Moravi' is terrific if you can track it down and 'Moneymaker' will produce reliably.

Very large or beefsteak varieties need a long growing season and plenty of sunshine. They probably do best in southern parts of the country. 'Brandywine' is a favourite one for making superb tomato sauce.

☑ It's hard to recommend lots of new varieties, since these can change on a yearly basis. The best tip for choosing varieties is to ask local growers. They will know what does well on your soil and what isn't worth the time.

☑ Even if you have favourites, it is worth trying new varieties and 'resting' one of the old ones every year. This helps keep crops productive and disease free. You might also find a new favourite variety for years to come.

Peppers

Peppers can do really well in an unheated polytunnel. Both chilli and sweet varieties do best if sown by the end of February or, at latest, the middle of March. If it gets much later than that, buy plants from a garden centre in a few weeks' time. Fresh seed can take up to three weeks to germinate and old seed can take a week longer again, so it can be well into March before seedlings appear. This allows just enough growing time for plants to get big enough to plant out at the end of May.

Peppers seem to do best if sown singly in pots. If you are using new seed, pretty well all of it should germinate. Keep the temperature between 20 and 25°C/68 and 77°F, if possible, and be prepared to wait up to three weeks for the seedlings to emerge. There are lots of varieties available and everyone has their own favourite for shape, colour and hotness. New varieties appear each year, but early cropping ones are best for polytunnel growing. 'Gypsy' needs a mention – it performs well even in a poor year, giving exceptional crops of pale green fruits that ripen to orange and red. 'Bendigo' produces good solid fruit, 'Tasty Grill' grows 25cm/10in-long fruits and 'Sweet Nardello' has long slim fruit that twists to produce a spectacular-looking plant.

Aubergines

There is still time to start aubergines this month, but choose an early variety and sow as soon as possible.

Aubergines sown last month should be up by now and will be ready to prick out into individual 8cm/3in pots. Use a knitting needle to tease out roots and be careful not to damage the stems. If seedlings are 'leggy', make a hole and drop them down into the compost until the leaves just rest on the surface. Firm the compost gently around the stem. Keep aubergine plants in a propagator or on a warm, sunny window ledge for the time being. These plants hate low temperatures and chilly drafts.

Melons

Sow melons in late February, if continuing heat can be guaranteed. If they are to be grown on in an unheated structure, however, it might be safer to be patient for a while longer. The variety 'Sweetheart' is most likely to produce a successful crop.

Sow six seeds per 12cm/5in pot. Cover the pot with a plastic bag and keep at 20–25°C/68–77°F until seedlings poke through. Don't exclude light.

☑ The most prolific melons that I have ever grown were sown in February and raised in large pots in a sunny window ledge until I planted them out at about 45cm/18in tall. If you can give plants this sort of care, early sowing is fine.

Salad crops

Keep sowing salad crops at regular intervals for a continuous supply – a sowing every month seems about right. **Rocket** grows quickly at this time of year. Sow 1cm/½in-deep rows, in soil enriched with compost. Leaves should be ready for first pickings in about six weeks.

Continue sowing spring and summer varieties of **lettuce** in trays or pots. If sowing a row of **mixed salad leaves** directly into the border soil, read the packet carefully – **basil**, for example, won't be a success in an unheated polytunnel until temperatures rise.

RIGHT FROM TOP: Peppers; melon seedlings covered with a plastic bag; melons growing; salad crops

Keep sowing spinach

Peas in guttering for planting outdoors

Radishes will pop up quickly if sown now. Sow little and often for a regular supply.

Spinach or spinach beet

Sow a row of spinach or spinach beet this month. Both grow rapidly, producing tender young leaves, all ready to take over from the tatty overwintered ones in a few weeks' time. Spinach beet is a much easier crop to grow than spinach and is particularly good for beginners to try. A direct-sown and unthinned row will give plenty of small leaves, but plants will crop for only a few weeks. If you thin plants, or sow in a pot and plant out at 20cm/8in spacing, this allows plenty of room for individual plants to grow. Such plants can crop for many months, but leaves might grow too large and coarse for some tastes.

Both spinach and spinach beet like plenty of compost in the soil and plenty of moisture at all times. Add a scattering of hydrated lime or wood ash to the surface of an acid soil.

Kohl rabi

Seed sown now will provide juicy sweet roots in ten to twelve weeks' time. Try a mix of red-skinned and green-skinned varieties – it's easy to tell the seedlings apart. 'Azur Star', 'Noriko', 'Kohlibri' and 'Olivia' are all good varieties. Seed can be sown in a pot or tray. Just sow a pinch at a time and plan on growing maybe a dozen plants from one sowing. Kohl rabi can be sown at most times of the year for continuous crops, so don't waste the seed by sowing it all at once. Seedlings are pretty hardy and don't suffer ill effects from transplanting.

Outdoor sowings

A polytunnel isn't just for tomatoes and cucumbers: it can also be put to good use to help grow great outdoor crops. February is the month to sow **beetroot**, **leeks** and **celeriac** in cells or trays. Start a sowing of **peas** in a length of guttering, or **broad beans** in pots. **Brussels sprouts** do best from an early start; these can be raised in the polytunnel for planting outdoors, or they can be grown on in large pots until space clears for planting in the tunnel later in the year. These are all pretty hardy crops and they won't need the protection of a polytunnel in a few weeks' time, but this early start puts them ahead in the growing game. All these sowings will thrive with the extra protection and warmth that the tunnel provides.

Strawberries

Keep compost in strawberry pots moist. To test it, tap the side of the pot – a hollow sound means the compost is too dry, a dull sound indicates damp compost. Don't let temperatures rise too high at this stage; otherwise plants may grow lots of leaf at the expense of flowers.

Herbs

Herbs grown in containers in the polytunnel will be ready for use much earlier than ones grown outside. Chives get a really early start and they will keep going for most of the year. Parsley sown now will keep growing through the summer months and into the winter. Pots can be moved outdoors once the weather warms up.

Support for peas

Autumn-sown mangetout peas may be 25–30cm/10–12in tall by now. Push some small twigs into the soil on each side of the row. The pea tendrils will twirl around the twigs and the young plants will support themselves. They will need taller support, in the form of branches, netting or strings, as they grow. Don't leave plants to trail on the ground – the growing points will be eaten by slugs.

Parsley

Washing down the walls

The plastic covering a newly erected polytunnel is clear and clean, but after a year of use a coating of algae and dust starts to build up. After several years, the polythene can become so green and dingy that the amount of light getting through is low enough to restrict plant growth. Don't worry! A good wash-down can restore it to almost-new levels of clarity. This should be done once every year. Twice a year is even better, but realistically most people aren't that fanatical.

February is a good month to get scrubbing. The polytunnel isn't crowded with tall crops and it's a good idea to get polythene as clean as possible for the start of the growing year (see Part 6).

Don't forget the fittings and fixtures

Wooden benches often have gaps between the boards. These can be full of last year's potting mix, along with a few unwelcome visitors. Use a brush, knife or vacuum cleaner to remove the layer of unwanted debris. Scrub benches and shelves with warm soapy water (add Citrox or tea tree oil for a bit of extra sterilizing power).

If there are jobs you have ignored through the past few months, do them now

Order seeds, before favourite varieties sell out
Clear all dead or diseased plants and foliage
Wash all used pots and trays
Trim hedges or trees that put the polytunnel in the shade
Dig well-rotted manure, or compost, into empty borders
Mend broken doors, benches, shelves, etc. that will be working hard all year long

Warm the soil

Empty areas of the border can be covered with black polythene. This absorbs heat and will help raise the temperature of the soil underneath. Remove the polythene at planting time, unless your intention is to use it as a mulch.

Start collecting

February is a relatively quiet month in the polytunnel. It is worth starting to gather a few things together that will help ease the workload in the months ahead:

- Poles, sticks or canes for supporting plants, including some that are twiggy enough to support peas, some that are small to mark rows and some long enough for 2m/7ft-tall tomato vines
- Plastic 2-litre/3½-pint milk bottles, to make water reservoirs for thirsty plants
- Plastic fruit tubs for raising seedlings
- Clear-plastic water bottles for mini cloches
- Dry wood ash from the fire or bonfire for potash-greedy plants
- A tub of liquid feed (see Part 7) to give plants a boost
- Strong boxes, preferably of plastic or wood, to hold pots of growing plants
- Plenty of covering material to protect against low temperatures
- Clear plastic bubble wrap for insulating propagation trays

Enjoy the February harvest

Broccoli	Salad leaves
Kale	Oriental leaves
Swiss chard	Fennel
Spinach	Spring cabbage
Kohl rabi	Turnip
Lettuce	Beetroot
	Herbs

February harvest of Swiss chard, fennel, oriental leaves and salad leaves

Some harvesting hints

- The first shoots of **purple sprouting broccoli** will make an appearance in February. This can be several weeks ahead of an outdoor crop. Pick out the central spike once it has grown to a decent size and other shoots are growing well. Don't pick out all shoots at once; there should be an abundant supply of smaller shoots, lower down the stems, to follow on.
- **Swiss chard** should be cropping well and the leaves will be far more succulent than those outdoors. Use both leaves and stems, as both are delicious. Never strip a plant – just take a few large outer stems from each one.
- **Kohl rabi** can be picked at any stage from golf-ball size up to a decent tennis ball. Don't let them run to seed; otherwise they will become woody.
- The polytunnel should be flush with **fresh young leaves** – spicy mixtures of **oriental leaves** for cooking or eating raw, plus **spinach**, **lettuce** and **salad leaves** of all shapes and colours. You shouldn't be short of ingredients for a salad or stir-fry at this time of year.
- August sowings of **spring cabbage** will be filling out now and some will be ready for harvesting.
- Overwintered roots such as **turnip** or **beetroot** should be eaten small, while juicy and sweet.
- **Fennel** may look a bit tatty on the outside, but if plants have survived this long from an autumn sowing, it's what's on the inside that counts. Peel back outer layers and inside there will be a fresh clean bulb – such a delicious taste at this time of the year.

Purple sprouting broccoli

MARCH

March in the polytunnel is about laying the foundations for great summer crops. Young tomatoes, peppers and aubergines should be growing well and lots more seeds can be started in pots. In fact, the polytunnel can resemble a plant nursery. If this puts the gardener in the role of nanny, there's no harm in that – the future cropping potential of plants can be affected even at this early stage.

Weather report

March should bring drier weather than the previous two months, but it can also bring a wide range of conditions: through frost and snow to strong winds, heavy rain or bright sun. At this time of year the difference between the most northern gardens and southern ones can be three or four weeks. Always take this into account and if necessary defer sowing or planting until the soil temperature rises above 7°C/44°F in the polytunnel.

March jobs in brief

Keep sowing
Prick out and pot on
Pollinate broad beans
Provide support for peas
Mulch grape vines
Ventilate on any warm day

Water carefully
Think about companions
Clear finished crops
Watch out for pests
Earth up around potato stems

Propagation time

☑ If you intend to buy in small plants from seed companies, you have to order them in advance. Orders in early March might arrive in April and early April orders might arrive in May. Check the catalogues for last order dates.

Time to sow

Tomatoes	Rocket
French beans	Lettuce
Courgettes	Salad leaves
Basil	Kohl rabi
Cucumbers	Spinach
Melons	Peppers
	Aubergines

Make space for seedlings

Propagation is certainly the name of the game this month. Even if other jobs lag behind, keep up with the sowing and potting on. Buying in plants is, of course, another option, although there will be far less choice of varieties. Many seed suppliers and garden centres offer plants in small pots or as plugs. These will not have enough compost to sustain growth for very long, so should be potted on or planted out as soon as possible.

☑ Make your own plant labels from plastic milk bottles cut into strips. Once the plastic is washed and dried, you can use a permanent marker so that names don't fade.

A thought on raising plants from seed

It's strange that people who would happily grow most outdoor crops from seed are wary when it comes to polytunnel plants. It may seem a long way from a tiny seed to a 2m/7ft-tall vine dripping with tomatoes, but those seeds want to grow. It's what they are about after all! Germinating a seed and growing it until the young plant is just a few centimetres tall seems to be the easiest bit of the whole process, yet that is what you pay a plant supplier for. Why not give seed sowing a try and open the door to growing a wider range of varieties?

And a few on compost

It's wise to buy a few bags of compost early in March, while there is still plenty of choice. Home-made compost is always an option (see Part 7). This works very well for sowing large seeds like peas and beans, or for potting on larger plants, but you will need fine compost for starting small seeds.

TOP: Broad beans in flower
BOTTOM: Making plant labels

TOP: Open propagator
BOTTOM: Using a knitting needle to prick out tomatoes

☑ If it gets too hot during the day, open the cover of the propagator. This allows air to circulate and gives the best chance of raising healthy plants. A thermostat will switch the propagator off as temperatures rise, but it can't stop the effect of the sun's rays. When temperatures start to fall again replace the cover.

Peppers and aubergines

Both of these can still be sown in March. Choose early varieties like the aubergine 'Moneymaker' and the pepper 'Gypsy'. If you haven't sown seed by the end of March, it is best to find plants to buy instead.

Seedlings from earlier sowings will be growing well. Remove the polythene and keep them at 15–20°C/59–68°F. Pot on into larger pots if necessary.

Tomatoes

Tomatoes can be sown this month for summer crops (see February). Ones sown in trays last month will be ready for pricking out and potting on, and the same will apply to early March sowings before the month is out. This should be done when the seed leaves are open, but do take care: seedlings are fragile at this stage and stems can break. Always choose the strongest seedlings for growing on. Use a kitchen fork, or a knitting needle, to gently loosen the roots. Lift the seedling by the leaves, rather than the stem, and transfer it immediately, so that roots don't dry out. If tomato seedlings are a bit 'leggy' don't worry – make a hole deep enough to take most of the stem of the seedling. Leaves should just sit on the surface of the compost. Seedlings will grow quickly to produce sturdy little plants by the end of the month.

☑ Keep pots at a temperature of 15°C/59°F and out of strong sunlight for the first few days after transplanting. Once the seedlings are established they can be grown on in full sun, but try to keep the temperature around 15°C/59°F.

Courgette 'Parthenon'

Dwarf French beans

French beans sown in March should start to crop in June. Sow seed singly in small pots or multiple sow in larger pots. If the weather is cold, keep the pots indoors, or in a propagator at 15°C/59°F, until seedlings appear (this should take 5–7 days). After that, they shouldn't fall below 10°C/50°F.

Courgettes

Try sowing a couple of courgettes on a warm window ledge, or in a propagator set to 20°C/68°F. Do this at the beginning of March, and then sow a couple more later in the month just in case the early ones don't make it. This may seem very early to sow, but if plants are covered, so that they aren't exposed to frost, they will produce plenty of delicious small fruit by mid-May.

Courgette plants take up a lot of room in a polytunnel. They come into their own at the beginning and end of the season, or in a poor summer, when ones grown outdoors aren't cropping. Plants can always be evicted from the polytunnel if outdoor ones start producing well.

☑ I sow the variety 'Parthenon' for the earliest crops. The flowers don't require pollination in order to set fruit.

Basil

This herb ranks high on the list of polytunnel favourites. A dozen plants will provide plenty of leaves to eat fresh with tomatoes, and to make a few tubs of delicious pesto, but real basil addicts might want to grow more.

Early sowings produce large bushy plants, so it is worth starting in March. Choose a 'Sweet Genovese' variety to grow in the border for large, well-flavoured leaves. These make excellent pesto. Small-leaved varieties do well in large pots. Sow three or four seeds per module, if using cells, or scatter several over the surface of a larger pot. Basil likes its own company, so don't thin once seedlings emerge. Germinate at 20°C/68°F and keep young plants warm.

☑ I raise my seedlings in a sunny kitchen window, which gives better results than the propagator. I can't tell you why, but it works, so I stick with it!

Cucumbers

Cucumbers can crop in May from early March sowings, but they need a lot of care through the weeks in between. The main problem with early sowings is that cucumbers grow very fast and often produce large plants that outgrow the propagator. If the polytunnel is warm enough in late April or early May there is no problem, as plants can go straight into their final planting position. In a cold year, however, there may be a delay in planting out. Early sowings that are held in small pots for too long can be prone to root rot and large plants can collapse overnight.

To play safe, make two sowings: the first in early March and the second in April, or even May, to extend the season. Choose all-female varieties for the early sowing to avoid the task of picking out male flowers or the disappointment of bitter fruit.

Remember that the average family needs only two or three cucumber plants. Sow four or five seeds (one seed, 1cm/½in deep, per 8cm/3in pot) and keep at 20°C/68°F until seedlings emerge. This gives a couple of spare plants in case some don't make it.

Cucumber seedlings

☑ **or maybe not:** Plenty of people advocate sowing cucumber and melon seeds edge up, so that they shed water and don't rot. Plenty of other people say they get equally good germination from sowing seed flat. I'm really not sure about this, but cucumber seed can be expensive, so I tend not to risk losing it and sow sideways just in case!

Pricking out
melon seedlings

Melons

You can sow melons now, but keep them warm. Always choose an early variety that does well in an unheated polytunnel. 'Sweetheart' is probably the most successful variety for a beginner to try. Sow six seeds in a 12cm/5in pot. Cover with a plastic bag and keep at 20–25°C/68–77°F. Seedlings should emerge in a few days, but melons often have difficulty breaking free of the seed case. If this sticks to the first leaves, ease it away *very* carefully. Seedlings are delicate and it can be all too easy to break the stem. Try wetting the seed case to make it more pliable. Leave the plastic bag over the pot, and keep the pot in a warm, sunny place until all seedlings have emerged.

If you made a multiple sowing of melons last month, seedlings should be ready to be pricked out into individual 8cm/3in pots.

☑ I prefer not to bury too much stem when potting on melons and cucumbers. I recommend piling compost around the stem when plants are larger, but rot can be a real problem when plants are small.

Sowing without extra heat

Lettuce, salad leaves, rocket and **kohl rabi** will germinate without any extra heat. Make regular sowings if these are favourite crops. Lettuce can start off in pots, but small salad leaves are always best sown directly where they are to grow on.

It's still worth sowing a few early **carrots** in a 25cm/10in pot in the polytunnel at the beginning of March. These should produce young fresh roots a few weeks earlier than the ones sown outdoors. Earlier sowings should be well up this month – don't thin the seedlings, but do be extra vigilant for slugs and snails.

Peas and beans

Pea flowers are
self-fertile

If you sowed broad beans and mangetout peas in the polytunnel last autumn (or in January, for that matter), these should be growing rapidly now and they might start to flower. Keep the soil damp – a dry root run will reduce the number of flowers and hence limit the crop.

Push branches in either side of the pea row, or use netting or fencing wire, to provide enough support so that stems don't flop and break. Broad beans don't need much support in a polytunnel, but you can use sticks and string if plants start to flop. Make sure that supports don't rub against the polythene – a sharp stick might puncture it.

Both of these vegetables should crop very well under cover, but broad beans may need a little help with the pollination of first flowers. Leave a door open so that bees can find their way in, or try using a soft paintbrush. Peas are self-fertile and will set pods without any assistance.

Grapes

Tie the vine back on to support wires, if it was untied for the winter. Grape vines always appreciate a 5cm/2in-thick mulch of manure at this time of year. Weed first and make sure the soil is damp before applying any mulch.

Strawberries

For extra early crops, plants should have been under cover for a few weeks now. The earliest of all will be from the plants left to grow in the border soil and many may be in flower. A rub with a soft paintbrush will aid pollination and help avoid misshapen fruit.

Watch out for frost, which will blacken the heart of flowers as it kills them outright. Cover rows of flowering strawberries if the nights are cold. If low temperatures do their worst remove any affected flowers – more will grow to produce later fruit.

Air and water

Cautious ventilation is important now. Prop doors ajar, or fling them wide open if the sun shines and temperatures soar. A polytunnel can easily get up to 30°C/86°F on a bright day. Always close doors again in the evening when temperatures drop.

Water carefully when the soil begins to dry out. Flowering peas and beans will crop much better if you give them a plentiful supply of water and established crops need more than just the surface of the soil dampening. Seedlings should be watered with the utmost care and compost should never be soggy. Sometimes a spray over the leaves is the best way to cool a plant down on a hot day.

Companion plants

French marigolds and nasturtiums repel whitefly and keep greenfly away from other plants. It is worth sowing both, to help in the battle to keep pests away from polytunnel crops. Even if you find it hard to accept the idea of companion planting, these flowers will look attractive and make the polytunnel a lovely environment to work in.

Clearing crops

The end of March is time to start thinking about removing any flowering or bitter crops. There's no great rush, but these won't improve with more time in the ground and you will need the space for summer plantings next month.

Once plants set seed, they should be removed. Do this before they scatter their seeds all over the soil. If you are saving seed, choose the best plant to grow on and collect the ripe seed before it is dispersed. **Rocket** seed is easy to save, as it does not cross-pollinate with other brassicas. **Lettuce** seed is another easy one for beginners to save.

Strawberry flowers

Companion planting

TOP: Cut-and-come-again leaves
MIDDLE: Spring cabbage
BOTTOM: Cutting mibuna

Enjoy the March harvest

Spring cabbage
Sprouting broccoli
Lettuce
Kohl rabi
Spinach
Swiss chard
Kale
Fennel
Beetroot
Salad leaves

Some harvesting hints

The list of crops to harvest is pretty similar to that of the previous two months. There should be plenty to eat, as plants start to grow faster with the extra light and heat from the lengthening days.

- The new season's sowings will still be small. Be patient, and it won't be long before they come into their own.
- September-sown **fennel** and **beetroot** should be perfect for eating now if the winter hasn't been too harsh.
- **Rocket, mizuna** and **mibuna** will be bursting with leaves. Pick these before the plants try to flower and set seed.
- Give **spring cabbage** another feed of liquid manure and they should start producing a mass of tender leaves. Use the first plants while small; otherwise there may be too many to eat in a few weeks' time.
- **Sprouting broccoli** should still be cropping well under cover, but move it out once the spears become thin or start to flower.
- **Mustard greens** and **kales** can grow massive leaves in the protected environment of a polytunnel. They can also become strongly flavoured at this time of the year. Keep picking regularly to force plants to produce more, smaller leaves. Once the taste gets too strong, or the leaves are too tough, evict the lot.
- **Lamb's lettuce** seems to keep its subtle flavour even when the plants are about to bolt. Even so, winter sowings may be finishing up this month. Pick the row before plants flower.
- **Parsley** can be a winner at this time of the year. Plants reared under cover can provide plenty of pickings until the spring sowings take over in a few months' time.
- Keep harvesting **lettuce** and **salad leaves**. This is a regular job throughout the year, but not an unpleasant one!

APRIL

April is such a month of promise. Seedlings are growing fast and the weather might even be hot. Inside the polytunnel it will be warmer still. It's easy to imagine the space filled with melons and grapes, or to look at those small tomato plants and imagine picking a bumper crop. The next few weeks are crucial ones: plants get put out into the borders and growth steps up a notch or two. It can seem hectic at times, with lots of small tasks to attend to, but things will calm down before too long.

Weather report

April might bring showers and even snow, but the year is on the move. Sunshine levels are increasing and there is a strong possibility of some good hot days. Night frosts might disappear in some parts of the country by the end of the month, but don't be in too much of a hurry to declare the last frost passed – more can appear in May.

April jobs in brief

Water carefully

Open the propagator on warm days

Keep sowing

Keep potting on seedlings and small plants

Soak the subsoil before planting out

Harden off tomatoes and courgettes

Plant out tomatoes, courgettes and French beans

Feed strawberries

Organize growbags and pots

Aid pollination

Clear old crops

Open doors to provide ventilation

Replace old and torn polythene

Watch out for greenfly

Still plenty of overwintered greens

Sowing pumpkins

TOP:
Florence fennel
seedlings
BOTTOM:
Spinach
seedlings

Time to sow

Cucumbers	Kohl rabi
Sweetcorn	Basil
Pumpkins	Fennel
Climbing French beans	Marigolds
Spinach	Courgettes
Tomatoes	Broccoli
Salad leaves	Sprouts
Lettuce	Kale

April sowings and buying in plants

• Seed sown in April should germinate quickly and seedlings usually suffer fewer setbacks to growth as temperatures start to settle. Plants won't quite catch up with February and early March sowings and so will not produce the earliest crops, but they won't be too many weeks behind.

• If you haven't sown **peppers** and **aubergines** by now, it is probably best to buy in plants. These stand the best chance of producing a summer crop. There is still time to try sowing **melons** at the beginning of April, but only if using a fast, early and reliable variety, like 'Sweetheart'. If the summer is hot these will bear fruit. Otherwise, buy plants and keep them warm until they are ready to go out.

• **Tomato** seed can be sown up until the end of April, but it might be best to buy in a few plants of medium or large varieties. Early April sowings of cherry varieties will start to crop in mid- to late summer and may well give the best autumn fruit.

• Sow **basil** if you didn't do so in March. In fact, it can be wise to make a second sowing in April just in case anything goes wrong with the March sowing and you need a few extra plants.

• Try sowing **Florence fennel** in small pots or cells around mid-April. This crop gets off to a great start in the polytunnel. Put two seeds in each pot – you will thin these later to leave the strongest seedling to grow on. For good germination fennel needs a bit of heat, but not too much (12–15°C/54–59°F is fine). If nights are cold, germinate seed inside the house, or find a space at the edge of the propagator. This sowing will usually be destined to grow on outdoors, but summer sowings of fennel can be grown on in the polytunnel.

• **Climbing French beans** will stretch up to the roof. Sow early in April for plants that will keep cropping right through the summer and even into October. Climbing French beans come in a variety of colours. Sow a few each of purple, green and yellow varieties for a really attractive display. 'Blauhilde', 'Neckar Queen' and 'Goldfield' will give the full range.

• In a large polytunnel, it makes sense to sow **lettuce** and rows of **salad leaves** right through the summer. If the tunnel is small, however, save the space for more exotic crops and grow salad outdoors. The same applies to **spinach** and **kohl rabi**, although both of these do exceptionally well in a polytunnel.

• Early April is the best time to sow **sprouting broccoli, kale** and **Brussels sprouts**. These plants will not find a permanent home in the polytunnel until much later in the year, and in the meantime they will have to grow on in large pots outside the tunnel door. Sowing in April will give the fastest-cropping, largest plants, but May or even June sowings will still give good crops. For a simpler option, buy in plants in plugs in a few weeks' time.

Careful watering

All plants need water, but too much can be as bad as too little. Waterlogged seedlings will collapse and disease is always a danger; even mature plants hate a soggy root run. It's best to assess how much more water a pot really needs, rather than soaking at random with a hosepipe. Push a finger into pots, or lift them up to check how damp the compost is around the drainage holes. Peat-based composts tend to dry out on the surface while the underneath might still be damp. On the other hand, propagators heat from underneath, so the bottom of the pot may be dry even though top layers are damp.

As a rule, small plants usually do better if kept slightly dry rather than soggy. This is especially true for **cucumbers** and **melons** – too wet a compost will lead to collapse. **Tomatoes** are an exception: stand pots in a bucket of water, from time to time, so that the compost is thoroughly wetted from the bottom up.

Keeping plants warm

Most tender plants such as **peppers**, **aubergines**, **cucumbers** and **melons** will suffer if the temperature falls below 10°C/50°F. Ideally, to crop at their best, they shouldn't be exposed to temperatures below 15°C/59°F, but this can be hard to guarantee. **Tomatoes** are a little hardier and can cope at 12°C/54°F quite happily (or even lower once they get their roots into the soil). Remember: you can carry vulnerable plants in pots indoors at night and put them back out in the polytunnel in the morning when things warm up. This ensures that they have plenty of light and adequate warmth in the absence of a propagator. It may seem like a lot of work, but it's only for a short while until outdoor temperatures settle down.

Tomatoes and **courgettes** can be left out of the propagator from the middle of the month if night-time temperatures are above 12°C/54°F. This will help harden them off, and it will also free up propagator space for other plants. If space is needed, and temperatures aren't reliably high at night, use a cloche to cover the plants. Drape an old duvet or blanket over the top at night and temperatures won't fall too low underneath.

Propagator full of small plants

Once you put plants out into the border soil, the stems and leaves have to suffer what fluctuations of air temperature are thrown at them, but the roots will be kept at a more steady temperature in the soil. If nights are cold, cover rows of plants, or wrap a few sheets of newspaper, a sack, or a piece of fleece around individuals, but remember to remove coverings during the day.

Remember to open the propagator to keep temperatures from getting too high on sunny days. Close it at night to keep plants warm.

Young cucumber plants

Cucumbers

It is worth making a second sowing of cucumbers in April. Sow single seeds 1cm/½in deep per 8cm/3in pot. These will grow rapidly to give a good summer crop. A sowing this month safeguards against any failure of earlier plants. Try an all-female variety like 'Tiffany' or 'Flamingo'; or for a less temperamental option try 'Burpless Tasty Green', which produces male flowers, but they don't have to be removed, so there is no extra work attached.

Young plants from March sowings should be growing rapidly. Be fanatical about keeping the compost on the dry side of damp, in order to avoid root rot, and keep potting on into larger pots rather than risk a crowded root system in a small pot.

It isn't usually warm enough to plant cucumbers out in an unheated polytunnel in April. However, if plants go into a hotbed (see May) and if night temperatures are above 12°C/54°F you can plant cucumbers out at the end of the month. If temperatures are much lower than this, keep plants warm and wait until May.

Sweetcorn

The first sowings this month will give ripe cobs in late July and early August. Make a second sowing three weeks later for a staggered crop. Cross-pollination between some varieties can lead to poorly filled cobs and in supersweet varieties the kernels can be less sweet. To avoid this, sow one variety at a time. Most modern varieties produce well-filled cobs with yellow kernels. Try the variety 'Indian Summer' for multicoloured cobs and a really sweet flavour.

Sweetcorn needs a bit of warmth for good germination, but avoid cold wet compost, as otherwise seedlings will flop. Sow one seed 1cm/½in deep per 8cm/3in pot, or use root-trainers. Sweetcorn puts down long roots, so anything you use for raising seed should be as deep as possible. Keep at 20°C/68°F until shoots appear, and then try to maintain a temperature above 12°C/54°F.

Pumpkins and squash

Sow a couple of pumpkins (or squash) at the same time as sowing sweetcorn. Sow more if you plan to raise extra plants for growing outside. Pumpkins can take up a lot of room, but less so if they are twined among the growing stalks of corn. The pumpkin foliage covers the ground and keeps it moist – a bonus for the corn.

Sow each seed on its side in a 12cm/5in pot. Plants grow quickly and a large pot saves potting on.

Varieties that can be slow to fruit outdoors can do really well in a polytunnel. Try 'Butternut Squash' and 'Uchiki Kuri', or 'Small Sugar' for the most fruit of all.

Soak the subsoil before planting out

Soil can really dry out in the borders of a polytunnel, and especially so if these have been left empty and unwatered for several months. A sprinkling of water over the top of dry soil can run through without wetting, or it will simply dampen the surface layer. Some plants, like tomatoes and sweetcorn, can grow extensive root systems that will search for the essential moisture, but it is important to provide them with a good starting stock. So take a little time to get the subsoil thoroughly wetted before planting out thirsty crops.

To do this, dig a hole about 30cm/12in wide and deep for each plant. Fill this with water, let it drain and then fill it again. Repeat this until the subsoil is thoroughly soaked, as well as the surface layers. Do this about a week before planting tomatoes to allow excess water to drain before you put young plants out. At planting time the hole will be filled with damp compost, but by then the surrounding soil will have a store of water that will last for weeks.

The same technique can be used with plants grown in a trench. Simply fill with water, and allow to soak before refilling again.

Tomatoes

These are the main polytunnel crop for many people. They can be spectacular producers and the taste of a home-grown tomato is quite superb. Success with this crop depends on the variety to a certain extent. It depends much more on how plants are fed and watered, and if they have adequate support and enough room for air and light to circulate. You can establish good patterns for all these with good planting techniques.

☑ I always plant my tomatoes out into an unheated polytunnel by the end of April. I also always dither about the exact date, wondering if it is warm enough, if plants are big enough and if they have been hardened off enough. The answer to all these, in my garden, is always yes. The tomatoes not only survive but also thrive once they get their roots down into a rich damp medium and I have never lost any. The secret is good soil preparation and strong plants. Of course a lot depends on how far north you live. If in doubt, ask a local, experienced gardener. You should also prepare a stack of materials (newspaper, crop cover, woven sacks, etc.) to wrap around individual plants if nights get cold.

Soaking the subsoil

Tomato plants can be spectacular producers

Secure the lower end of support strings by tying round the root ball

Harden off tomato plants

Young tomato plants should have been out of the propagator during the day for a few weeks before planting out. You need to wean them off night-time propagator heat as well. Do this when night temperatures seem settled and not too cold. Plants should never be exposed to sudden jumps in temperature; use fleece, cloches, etc., if necessary, to acclimatize them to lower temperatures.

Preparing the bed and planting out tomatoes

• Dig manure into the bed well in advance of planting, if possible. Then dig out large planting holes, fill with water and allow to drain until the subsoil is soaked (see above).
• Push a support cane or stick into the soil at the bottom of each hole. Use a crowbar if necessary, so that you can push the cane well down. Sticks and canes need to be long enough to support tall tomato plants, but they mustn't rub against the polythene. They also need to be strong enough so that they won't break or bend under the weight of the crop. String is an alternative to canes: simply wind this around the root ball when planting and tie the other end up to the frame of the polytunnel. However, this method works only if tomatoes are to be grown beneath the hoops of the frame, or if you string a wire between the hoops, so that you can tie the strings in.

☑ String made from natural fibres may rot and break under the weight of the crop. For a strong support man-made fibres are a safer bet.

• Fill each planting hole with compost or well-rotted manure. Add a bit of dried seaweed, or wood ash, to provide extra potash for these greedy plants.
• Tomato plants should be 15–20cm/6–8in tall at planting time. They should have strong-looking stems and deep green leaves. Reject any spindly or discoloured plants. A very slight tinge of yellow isn't too bad: this means the plants have exhausted the compost in the pot and are ready to move on.
• Tip the root ball out of the pot and check that the roots look healthy. If roots have wound around the pot, tease them free so that they can gain easy access to the new planting medium.
• Allow plenty of room between plants: 45cm/18in apart in the row is fine, but allow at least 75cm/30in between rows. If rows are closer, plants must be further apart in the row.
• Young plants should be tied to the canes or strings to support the growing stem. Do this roughly every 30cm/12in as the plant grows. Don't pinch out side shoots until the young plants have established themselves in their final home – the side shoots won't adversely affect growth if left in place for the first week after planting out.
• Tomatoes can be planted into growbags, or 25cm/10in pots, with great success. Cut slits in the bottom of a growbag, so that roots can work their way down to the soil beneath. This isn't essential, but a sealed bag means you have to pay greater attention to watering and feeding all summer long.
• Another way to boost feeding power is to cut large round holes in the growbags and

push 20cm/8in pots (with plants) into these. Roots will grow down through the pot and into the growbag.

Planting tomatoes

NOTE: If conditions aren't right for planting out, always pot up into a larger pot rather than risk restricting growth.

Planting French beans

Dwarf varieties, sown in pots last month, can be planted out as soon as they have two proper leaves, but wait a little longer if temperatures are below 8°C/46°F. Plant in a double row over a trench filled with compost, the rows 20cm/8in apart, and allow 15cm/6in between each plant. Move as much of the root ball as possible without damaging roots. If the soil is acidic, scatter a little hydrated lime, or wood ash, over the soil around the plants.

> ☑ I find that French beans can survive temperatures as low as 5°C/41°F, if a cold night comes out of the blue, but the plants will die if temperatures dip much below this. A double layer of fleece is usually enough to keep plants safe on cold nights.

Planting courgettes

Courgettes sown last month can be planted out in mid-April. Allow plenty of space for the plants to grow – they often get much larger than ones grown outdoors. Dig a hole about 30cm/12in square and deep. Thoroughly wet the subsoil (see page 61) before filling the hole with compost. Courgettes are thirsty plants, so it is worth leaving a slight depression around the young plant. This will act as a reservoir when you water in the months ahead.

Use a stick to mark where a courgette is planted

☑ Always put a stick in the ground to mark where the stem goes into the ground. By the time the courgette plant is fully grown it can be hard to find the best point to water among all those leaves.

Courgettes are cold sensitive, but far less so than some other plants. Air temperatures can go down to 5°C/41°F in the tunnel with no obvious setback, provided this doesn't persist for more than two or three nights. If the night is to be really cold, throw an extra layer of fleece over the plants and they should be fine. Better still, to maintain steady growth, cover the plant with a large, clear plastic tub or container. This will act as an easily removable cloche.

☑ If space is limited, try growing a courgette plant in a large pot or bucket and move this outdoors once the weather warms up.

Potting on aubergines and peppers

These plants grow slowly and at times it may look as if they haven't moved much at all. Check to see if roots are restricted in the pot and if that's the case pot them on. Aubergines and peppers won't go out into an unheated polytunnel until well into May, or even June, but growth mustn't be held back in the meantime. These will probably be the last plants to leave the propagator – they really do need heat if they are to flower early and to crop well.

Aubergine plants ready to pot on

While handling each plant, give it a health check. A little attention now may help avoid future problems. Watch out for greenfly, which seem to be particularly fond of young pepper plants. If you spot that leaves are curled or distorted, this could be the problem. Squash the greenfly between finger and thumb, or take the plants outdoors and give them a good squirt of water to dislodge the pests. The fallen greenfly will stay outdoors when you return the plants to the tunnel. This is safer than using chemicals on sensitive young plants.

Planting out lettuce

Plant out lettuce, spinach and kohl rabi

If you sowed these in pots in February or early March, they will be ready to plant out when 3–5cm/1¼–2in high. Make drills about 5cm/2in deep in the border soil. Mark the row with sticks and string. Fill each drill almost to the top with compost. Lift each plant carefully, keeping the roots intact. Firm them into the compost-filled drills, allowing 15–20cm/6–8in between plants and 25–30cm/10–12in between rows.

☑ If you plant lettuce in blocks, be sure to allow enough access at each side. You should be able to reach in to weed, or to pick, without trampling on the growing plants.

Outdoor crops

Leeks and **celeriac** sown in February will have produced a flush of healthy seedlings by the beginning of April. These should be pricked out and potted on into deep tubs of compost. There is no need to keep them in the polytunnel once they are established, but it is best to keep them just outside the door. That way you can pop them back inside until fully hardened off.

Small **beetroot** plants in cells should be put outside to harden off at the start of the month. These will soon be ready to plant in an outdoor bed. Try growing a few inside the polytunnel if there is space – they will be ready a few weeks before the outdoor crop.

Feed strawberries

Plants in pots appreciate a liquid feed while the fruit is swelling. Apply this every seven days to give the best chance of growing lots of large, juicy strawberries. Try using a liquid feed made from comfrey and horse manure. Liquid seaweed works well too.

Don't let pots dry out at this point, as if you do the fruit will be small and poorly formed. Check leaves for mottling caused by virus disease and remove any severely affected plants, which will never crop well and may infect other healthy plants.

In a warm spring, a few fruits may ripen at the end of the month. Enjoy!

Strawberry plants in flower

☑ You may need to use netting to protect ripe fruit from adventurous birds, which will fly in through open polytunnel doors or squeeze under closed ones.

Grape vines

If you didn't feed vines last month, it's not too late to do the job now. A layer of manure, as a mulch around the stem, is the best way to provide a good supply of nitrogen.

New young shoots will grow rapidly. On newly planted vines, nip out the growing points of all except the lead shoot. This should be done after the side shoots have made six leaves.

Think about where to train the vine. Up and along the ridge is usually the best choice, provided it doesn't create too much shade.

Crops in containers

Carrots should be growing well in their containers and putting up plenty of leaf. Once carrot foliage is around 10cm/4in tall, slugs seem to leave it alone. Keep the carrot pot watered and fed while the young roots swell.

Potatoes in buckets need earthing up around the stem as the foliage grows. The bucket will be only half full of compost at planting time. March and April should be the right time to top up January and February sowings. Fill up to the top with compost, leaving just enough room to make watering easy. When filling the tub hold stems aside so that they aren't damaged, and try not to bury leaves – a good clump of foliage must remain above soil level. If necessary, earth up in two stages as the foliage grows.

Early crops may be ready to harvest.

First flowers on tomato plants

Think about pollination

Tomato plants can start to flower at the end of April. Mist them lightly with water around midday. This helps to set the first trusses of fruit.

Mangetout peas sown last October should be covered in flowers in April. The occasional bee might show an interest, but peas are self-pollinating, so don't need any insect help.

Strawberry flowers do need pollinating. If there are no suitable insects doing the job, use a soft fluffy paintbrush to transfer pollen. Incomplete pollination will lead to misshapen fruits.

Broad beans don't need any help outdoors, but they give a better set of early pods in a polytunnel if the plants are near an open door. A paintbrush might help, but it can be hard to get a brush into the flowers.

Make room for summer crops

Remove any crops that have finished producing, or have gone bitter, as the space will be needed for summer crops. It's still not too late to dig some well-rotted manure, or compost, into the beds after crops clear. Now is the time to decide which crops have finished and can easily be removed, and which will grow on to provide pickings for a few more weeks.

Check over rows of overwintered salad crops. Tear a leaf off and taste it! Some lettuce can turn horribly bitter and some of the oriental salad mixtures can get quite hot. Most leaves get tougher the larger they grow. For an extra spicy flavour, the leaves of crops like rocket and mustard greens can still be picked even when the plants are in full flower.

A bit of fresh air

Ventilation is really important in April. Avoid cold draughts, but try to prevent temperatures rising much above 30°C/86°F. This will mean judicious opening of doors on any sunny day. If it's windy outdoors, but temperatures are rising in the polytunnel, open the most sheltered door and use a heavy weight to stop it flapping. Always make sure that wind has a way to get out of the polytunnel if it blows straight in.

A new cover for the tunnel?

It may be the last thing that anyone wants to think about when the polytunnel is full of young plants, but April is about the best time to replace a polythene cover. If you leave this job until much later, the tunnel will be filled with large crops. Do it any earlier and the temperature will be too cold to ensure a good fit.

It is always best to choose a warm, calm, dry day for replacing polythene. This means the polythene is supple and expanded. Get the best fit possible on a warm day and when temperatures drop the polythene will shrink back to an even tighter fit. This helps avoid 'floppy polythene syndrome' and so can extend the life of the covering.

Enjoy the April harvest

First mangetout peas
First broad beans
Salad leaves
Lettuce
Spring cabbage
First strawberries
Kohl rabi
Spinach
Swiss chard
Sprouting broccoli
Oriental leaves
Beetroot
Baby carrots from autumn sowings
First early potatoes from December planting

TOP: Mangetout peas
MIDDLE: Broad beans
BOTTOM: April harvest

Some harvesting hints

- **Mangetout peas** sown last autumn should be covered in flowers in April, as should broad beans. Keep plants well watered while they are in flower. The first pods will be ready for picking from the middle of the month onwards. Pick while these are small and more will keep coming. The first pods are lovely raw in salads.
- **Spring cabbage** comes into its own and fills the traditional 'hungry gap', although of course there shouldn't be any gap at all if you have made regular sowings in the polytunnel. Use cabbage while the leaves are tasty and tender; if these are left too long the outer leaves become tough.

- **Kohl rabi** should be used at tennis-ball size or smaller. They will still be juicy and full of nutty flavour at this stage, but may run to seed as temperatures rise.
- **Swiss chard** 'Bright Lights' will keep cropping through the month, lending a splash of colour. Use both leaves and stems.
- **Spinach** may look tatty but it will keep producing until the new sowings take over.
- And, of course, there should always be plenty of **salad leaves**.
- **Sprouting broccoli** should have been cropping for several weeks at this stage. Make a last picking before evicting exhausted plants.
- **Beetroot** will be coming to an end from an autumn sowing. Pick and eat before plants bolt and the roots turn stringy.

MAY

May is often the nicest month of the year. There is heat in the sun and everything grows with an enthusiasm that is hard to match. The beginning of May is a busy time for the polytunnel gardener, with young plants jostling for attention and space. Remember your planting plan. Try to rotate crops even in a small space. Use growbags and containers if the soil is likely to carry disease. Cold nights might still be an issue, but don't panic: the workload will ease up by the end of the month as temperatures settle down and all those plants in small pots get settled into a more permanent home.

Weather report

May can be one of the driest and sunniest months of the year, but there are no guarantees! Watch out for late frosts this month. Temperatures of less than 5°C/41°F can do serious damage to tender plants raised in the expectation of heat. If days are bright and fine, nights are often clear and cold. Frosts can be at their worst around the full moon, particularly if this falls early in May. Once this has passed, it might well take the last frost with it.

May jobs in brief

Track down plants if extra are needed
Keep sowing for late summer and autumn crops

Clearing old crops makes room for new ones

Tie tomatoes in to supports and nip out side shoots
Mist early blossom to aid fruit set
Plant out tomatoes, sweetcorn, pumpkins, cucumbers
    and basil
If it is warm enough, plant peppers, aubergines
    and melons
Eat ripe strawberries!
Remember to water grape vines
Tie vines so that they don't touch the polythene
Grow climbing French beans to provide a bit of shade
Plant marigolds to protect tomatoes from whitefly
Harvest regularly
Clear the last of overwintered crops
Ventilate and water to maintain optimum conditions
Damp everything down on hot days

Lettuce seedlings

Time to sow

Cucumber	French beans
Sweetcorn	Lettuce and salad leaves
Basil	Kohl rabi
Pumpkins	Spinach

Thoughts on May sowings

The polytunnel might be almost completely planted up by the end of this month, but there are still one or two important crops that can be started now.

• If **cucumber** plants have collapsed through cold or root rot there is still time to sow seed in May. Try sowing 'Burpless Tasty Green', singly in 12cm/5in pots. Keep these at a steady temperature of 15–20°C/59–68°F and watch them grow. They won't bear fruit as quickly as earlier sowings, but the plants will certainly get full marks in the growing race. By the time August comes around, there will be as many cucumbers on these plants as on the ones sown in March.

• May brings a last chance to sow **basil** and almost the last to sow **sweetcorn** to give late crops. Sweetcorn does best from April or May sowings, but remember that cobs from one sowing tend to all become ready within a few days of one another. Some people love this and invite all their friends for a fresh sweetcorn feast. Another option is to make two sowings – one in April and another in May. This will give a staggered crop. Sow sweetcorn in the place where it is to grow now, so that the long roots can grow unrestricted into the ground.

• There's no problem in sowing a **pumpkin** in May to grow on in the polytunnel. Sow *in situ* and it will grow so fast that it might even catch up with April-sown ones.

• Keep sowing **dwarf French beans**. These crop really heavily under cover. It is well worth having a few short rows if space permits.

• Make regular sowings of **rocket** and other **salad** cut-and-come-again crops. These will be ready to cut in a few weeks. Don't cherish plants once leaves become straggly or bitter; the idea is to have a fast turnover of tasty leaves. These crops can be sown outdoors now, but they will grow faster, and suffer less damage, in the polytunnel.

- If **kohl rabi** is a favourite, make regular sowings, but if space is short, save this for a winter crop.

Acquiring young plants

Garden centres will stock some vegetable plants, but they may not have many tomatoes, peppers, cucumbers or aubergines left in May. Some seed companies also supply plug plants and although these should have been ordered in advance over the last couple of months, it might be worth phoning round if things are desperate. Another option is to ask a greenhouse or polytunnel grower near by: they might be happy to find a good home for a few surplus plants.

Health check before planting

All plants should be checked over before you plant them out in the polytunnel, and always choose the strongest ones for growing on. (This also applies when buying plants at a garden centre.) Height isn't always the issue – a shorter, well-coloured plant with a strong stem is often the best choice. Having said this, some weak-looking plants can go on to perform miracles once they get their roots into a decent growing medium.

French marigolds keep whitefly away from tomatoes

 Watch out for disease. If a young pot-grown plant is already showing signs, dispose of it. Keep only healthy plants in the polytunnel.

Planting out

Once temperatures settle down – often around the middle of May, or after the month's full moon has passed – you might judge it safe to plant out tender plants. This can be a tricky time to gauge, but at some point it comes down to just going for it. Plants in small pots are vulnerable, since the compost can get too warm and damp, or dry out too quickly. It is better to get plants into the border soil, or large pots, and hence provide a more stable environment for the roots. If this means covering with fleece, so be it.

 Become a weather fanatic and keep an eye on forecasts from day to day. Knowing what the next week has in store might influence your planting plans.

 If you have grown a few spare plants, leave these in pots. You might need them to replace any that fail from early planting.

Tomatoes

If you haven't already planted out tomatoes into their final home, do so in May (for planting technique, see April). Remember to plant a row of French marigolds near tomatoes to keep whitefly away. Plants begin to flower this month – try to avoid pot-bound specimens struggling into bloom.

Tomatoes are surprisingly tolerant of lower temperatures, so don't worry too much if temperatures dip down on the odd cold night. However, if temperatures below 10°C/50°F are forecast, it's worth providing a little extra protection. Wrap a sack, bag or bit of fleece around each plant in the evening and remove it in the morning once the sun has warmed things up.

Tomatoes in pots should be watered from the base. Stand them in a trough or large tub. The worst problems occur when the top layer of compost is damp: it gives the illusion of being adequately watered, but roots may be dry.

☑ Tomatoes are thirsty plants and I like to sink a cut-off milk carton or plastic drink bottle into the soil next to each plant. This makes watering a much faster job in the summer months.

Tomato side shoots

Most polytunnel tomatoes are trained as a single stem up a cane or string. However, they will try to grow into more bushy plants and so produce side shoots. If these shoots are left to grow on, plants will grow lots of leaf at the expense of fruit. Look in the joints where leaves meet the main stem. Cut, or nip out, any small shoots as soon as they appear there. Check for larger side shoots that have grown unnoticed. Larger shoots will make a bigger wound, so use a sharp knife or scissors to cut them out, leaving as clean a cut as possible. You can nip out smaller shoots between finger and thumb. It's worth checking every couple of days and removing side shoots while small. A large wound can allow disease to enter the plant.

Nipping out a tomato side shoot

☑ Always check round the base of the stem. New shoots will keep appearing there.

If you grow plants up canes, you should tie them in every 30cm/12in or so. Ties should be loose enough to allow the stem to expand as it grows, but not so loose that they slide down the cane. If you use strings for support it is possible to twist the stem around the string as it grows. An occasional tie will be needed to prevent a laden stem from slipping down.

Bush varieties don't need to be supported to the same extent (nor do they need to have side shoots removed). These varieties perform well in growbags, or large pots, and can be moved outdoors for the summer months; they don't make use of the space in a polytunnel in the same way that taller varieties do.

Tomatoes: early flower set

Cherry varieties of tomato produce plenty of flowers in May, but there can be problems in getting these earliest flowers to set fruit. Later trusses set without a problem, but the first ones may need a little help. This doesn't mean going around with a paintbrush, since the flowers will self-pollinate, but you can aid the process by adjusting humidity a little. Mist plants overhead with a fine spray of water in the morning and again in the evening. This ensures the pollen is just slightly damp (not saturated) and most likely to

First fruit set on a tomato truss

TOP: Sweetcorn ready to plant out
BOTTOM: Pumpkin and squash plants

set fruit. This won't be necessary for second and subsequent trusses, but the first ones always benefit from a helping hand.

With luck, the first green fruit should start swelling in May. Use a high-potash liquid feed, such as one based on seaweed, once a week through the next few months.

☑ Always dilute liquid feeds with plenty of water and never apply them to dry soil.

Sweetcorn

Sowings made last month will be ready for planting out in May. Sweetcorn puts down long roots and doesn't like anything that hinders that process. Because of this, it is best to get pot-grown plants into the border as soon as possible.

☑ Sweetcorn never does as well if grown in containers, but if you want to try it, choose the deepest ones you can find.

Plants should be planted 30cm/12in apart in each direction. Such close planting is fine if the plants are away from the polythene sides, but use a mulch so that it isn't a struggle to remove weeds in between. Planting in blocks aids pollination and helps ensure full cobs. Put plenty of well-rotted manure, or compost, into each hole at planting time. Don't stint on this and don't stint on water either – fill and refill the hole with water before planting so that it can drain to wet the subsoil. Sweetcorn is a greedy and thirsty plant, but if treated well it can produce two cobs (or sometimes three) per plant.

Plants from one sowing will all crop within a short time. If you want to extend the cropping season, make a second sowing in May.

☑ When planting corn apply a scattering of dried seaweed on the surface of the soil.

Pumpkins and squash

If you sowed seed last month, plants will have grown to fill their pots and be ready for planting out towards the end of May. It is fine to sow this month, but sow two seeds where each plant will grow – you will thin these later to allow the strongest one to grow on. Pumpkins need a lot of room and they are greedy feeders. One or two plants would be the maximum that an ordinary polytunnel could cope with. Even then, it might be necessary to trim back foliage and train the stems to grow out through the door if things get really excessive.

Make a hole 30cm/12in square and the same depth, among the sweetcorn block, half fill this with compost, put the plant in and backfill with soil. It is a good idea to make a shallow dip all around the plant to help with watering. Use a long stick to mark the point where you planted the pumpkin. It may seem obvious now, but once lots of foliage grows it will be hard to find where to water.

> ☑ Butternut squash often does much better in a polytunnel than it does outdoors.

Cucumbers: planting out

It can be hard to decide when to plant out the first cucumbers. Cucumbers are not as hardy as tomatoes, yet not as delicate as aubergines. Early May is a good guess. This choice will be driven by the fact that March-sown plants can be 30cm/12in tall and starting to flower, or even fruit. Also, there is always the fear that large plants in pots can flop overnight if roots start to rot. Cucumber plants hate to be in a pot of warm soggy compost, so keep them fairly dry in the pot. The rot starts underneath and plants are often too far gone before you notice the signs. Once plants get their roots into the more balanced temperatures of a larger bed, rot is less of a problem.

TOP: Planting cucumbers in a hotbed
BOTTOM: Twist cucumber stems round strings as they grow

Cucumbers that have been raised in heat should be hardened off for a week before planting out. Too sudden a temperature drop could mean losing the lot. It might be warm enough in the polytunnel simply to spread the plants out during the day and to cover them over at night, but if temperatures are low, the plants will have to hop back into the propagator at night until things warm up.

Cucumbers can be planted into large pots (25cm/10in minimum) or growbags, but they perform best of all in a hotbed (see part 7). Put a layer of compost on top of a pile of fresh strawy manure and leave for a few days, so that the first burst of heat cools, before planting out the cucumbers (45cm/18in apart). This keeps the roots warm but well drained, which helps avoid problems with root rot. If nights get colder after you have planted cucumbers out, drape fleece over the bed for a little extra protection. You can raise the fleece on sticks to act like a cloche and contain some of the heat rising from the bed.

> ☑ If a hotbed isn't an option, at least make a mound of soil and plant the cucumber on top of this to aid drainage.

Supporting growing cucumber plants

As plants grow they will need some support. Push a stick into the ground next to each one and tie a string to this. Tie the other end of the string up to the frame of the polytunnel (or to a wire stretched between two hoops). You can twirl the growing cucumber stem around the string. An occasional tie will keep a laden plant from sliding down the string.

Alternatively, tie a stone to the lower end of the string to weight it.

Female cucumber flower and immature fruit

Cucumber flowers and fruit

February-sown cucumbers will certainly flower and might well produce fruit in May. Don't let a small plant bear large cucumbers too early. A good solution is to pick fruit while still quite small and let only one or two grow at a time. By June, the plants will be large and strong enough to carry a much heavier crop. Remember that many older varieties produce bitter fruit unless the male flowers are removed regularly. The seed packet should state if this is the case.

☑ February-sown plants will usually be at peak cropping from June through August. It is worth sowing more seed in early May to get plants that will be at their peak in September and October.

Hardening off peppers, aubergines and melons

These young plants are less cold tolerant than tomatoes and cucumbers, so wait until the weather is settled and cold nights have passed before planting them out. This might be in the latter half of May, or even into June. Never plant out directly from the propagator into an unheated polytunnel, as the shock caused by the drop in temperatures can set plants back. Always harden off in stages. Each stage will take a few days or longer – it is hard to be precise, as this is so weather dependent.

1. Uncover the plants in the propagator during the day. If temperatures drop, heat will still kick in from underneath. This stage might start as early as a warm March or April.
2. Lift the plants out on to a sheet of polystyrene during the day. This helps keep the pots at a steady temperature. Put them back in the covered propagator at night.
3. Lift the plants out during the day, as above, and leave them out, but covered with insulating material such as fleece or crop cover at night.
4. Put the plants in their final growing position. Still cover them at night if temperatures drop below 15°C/59°F.

Nothing will be gained by planting out too early. If nights are cold, keep these tender plants warm until night-time temperatures are reliably above 12°C/54°F and preferably closer to 15°C/59°F. This may mean waiting until June before leaving them out in an unheated structure.

Aubergines do well in growbags

☑ Covering tender plants with a cloche for a few weeks, or even for months, after planting out can provide extra heat to ensure good crops.

Aubergines

If aubergines haven't been a success in previous years, try planting two per organic growbag (or one per 30cm/12in pot). Slit the base of the bag and sit this on soil that you have enriched with manure or compost. The plants love the warm growbag compost for an early start, but the roots will find their way down into the enriched soil in the summer months.

If plants are to go in the border, try to get hold of some well-rotted horse manure. This can work wonders if dug into the soil before planting. Allow a minimum of 45cm/18in between plants.

Water aubergines at the base of the plant, rather than wetting the leaves and flowers. The exception to this is in really hot, dry weather, when red spider mite can get out of control in the polytunnel: aubergines are particularly susceptible to this pest and the best way to avoid it is to keep everything damped down.

TOP: Grow a chilli pepper plant in a pot
BOTTOM: Melon plant ready to pot on

Peppers

Sweet peppers can produce great crops when grown in the border soil. To grow well they like plenty of organic material and potash. The organic material holds moisture in the soil. Peppers are thirsty plants and they will not crop well if denied access to water. Dig in an equal mix of compost and manure if possible. Manure alone contains too much nitrogen and the plants will produce leaf at the expense of fruit. Compost alone can be too low in nitrogen and leaves will be pale and plants stunted. Add a scattering of seaweed meal to provide potash. Plants should be 45–60cm/18–24in apart, depending on the size of the variety. Push a support stick down into the soil at planting time. The plant can be tied into this as it grows.

Peppers can also be grown in large pots or growbags (one plant per 30cm/12in pot and two plants per growbag). Chilli varieties particularly like this treatment, but they will exhaust available nutrients around eight weeks after planting. Since plants can crop right through to December, it's important to feed them in the months ahead and to be vigilant about keeping compost moist during flowering to ensure good fruit set.

☑ Chilli varieties do really well in large pots. I always plant one small variety in a 30cm/12in pot. I grow this on in the polytunnel, but bring it indoors in October. This provides fresh peppers and a splash of colour in the house through the winter.

Melons

Melons seem to suffer most if temperatures fall too low. If the weather is settled and night-time temperatures in the polytunnel don't fall below 15°C/59°F, you can plant melons into the border soil, or three per growbag, or one per large pot. If there is any doubt about the weather, it is safest to keep the young plants growing with a little added heat. Pot on into larger pots if necessary and plant out in June, if that's what the weather dictates.

Dig some manure into the soil, and then heap up a small mound around 10cm/4in high, so that the planted melon is elevated a little. This provides a better drainage system for temperamental roots. Alternatively, fill a wooden frame with compost, or make a hotbed and plant melons in this. Plants can be planted 30cm/12in apart

if you intend to train the stem upwards – in which case make sure a string can be tied into the polytunnel hoops, or use a cane. If plants are to ramble over the ground they need a wider spacing (45cm/18in).

☑ I usually ignore advice to pinch out growing points on melon plants, as anything that delays fruiting means the plants may not get a long-enough season to produce ripe fruit.

☑ Root rot is a problem in a cold, wet root run and stems can rot at ground level. To avoid this, I make a small hole in the side of the mound and water into this. This technique gets water down around lower roots, but keeps compost drier at ground level.

Basil

It's a good idea to get plants into the soil as soon as the weather warms up. They can tolerate a little cold much better than a restricted root ball in a pot of warm compost can. In fact, healthy young plants may start to flop if they don't get planted out soon. Even if young plants struggle for a week or so after planting, they quickly pick up and grow on well.

Don't split up clumps of small plants. Basil likes company, so plant two or three together and allow 30cm/12in between clumps.

Soil for a good basil crop should be enriched with compost or well-rotted manure. Basil doesn't do so well on impoverished or heavy soils. Don't overwater; try to mimic the drier conditions of the Mediterranean, where basil grows so well.

Strawberries

There should be plenty of ripe fruit this month, but a lot depends on the amount of sun. If May is hot and dry, berries will ripen earlier than they will if the month is dull and grey. Pick fruit as it ripens and cover with netting if birds are getting into the polytunnel and pecking at the berries. Watch out for dogs and small children as well – both of these pinch strawberries! Remember to water and apply a weak liquid feed while the berries are swelling. If the compost dries out the plants will produce small hard fruit.

Always remove any berries that show signs of grey mould.

Grape vines

Keep the vine under control. It is better to cut out some shoots than shade the entire polytunnel with a mass of leaves. Tie the main shoot in as it grows, but allow enough length in the tie so that foliage hangs away from the polythene. Remember that grapes need lots of water. Ideally roots should be outside the structure and so benefit from rainfall, but if the weather is dry, water roots well for a good crop of juicy fruit.

Small clusters of embryo fruit should form on the vine during May. You will need to trim back the shoots that grow these in June.

French beans

The first French beans might be ready for picking by the end of May. Pods dangle under the leaves in clusters, so take a careful look. Pick pods while small and firm and plants should continue to crop for several weeks.

If you sowed climbing beans in pots last month, they will be ready for planting out now; or you can sow early in May for a slightly later crop.

Fill a trench with plenty of compost. Use some from the heap – it doesn't matter if it is part-rotted. Beans don't need a lot of nitrogen, but they do like a nice moist root run. If the soil is acid, scatter hydrated lime on it at planting time.

Plants of climbing varieties can be planted 20cm/8in apart in a single row. Push a stick into the ground next to each one and tie a string from this up to the roof structure. Beans will naturally twine around the string, but they may need a little help in getting started.

Climbing French beans need something to climb

☑ Some plants, such as lettuce, don't like too much direct sun. If you plant them in the shade formed by a curtain of climbing beans, they will grow better than if they are exposed to the full heat of the polytunnel.

Clear seeding crops

Any bolting overwintered crops should be pulled early in May to make room for new planting. Don't treasure those old greens for too long – there should be plenty of delectable fresh pickings coming in.

Interplanting is always an option until plants clear. This can even provide some protection to new plants that you put out in between the old.

Ventilation and temperature

Along with watering, ventilation rates top of the list for success when you are growing under cover. With no ventilation, temperatures can get high enough to kill plants. With too much ventilation, cold and wind chill will do the same job. Open and close doors as necessary to maintain a steady growing temperature. Try not to let this go over 30°C/86°F or under 15°C/59°F ideally (or 10°C/50°F more practically) and most polytunnel crops will grow very well.

Plants in small pots can be killed and even large plants, with roots in the earth, can wilt if temperatures reach 40°C/104°F, but the beginning of the month can still bring cold nights. Shut doors in the evening and open them in the morning to avoid dramatic temperature swings.

Watering

Correct watering is crucial to healthy growth. Keep borders damp, spray overhead to keep plants cool and, if it is really hot, water paths: as water evaporates it will cool things down.

OPPOSITE FROM TOP: Female melon flower with tiny fruit; planting basil; ripe strawberries; keep vines under control

Enjoy the May harvest

New potatoes
Baby carrots
Courgettes
Cucumber
Salad leaves
Lettuce
Strawberries
Mangetout peas
Broad beans
Kohl rabi
Spinach
French beans

Some harvesting hints

- There should be plenty of healthy vibrant **spinach** and **salad leaves** all bursting with the sweet taste of a fast-grown crop. If there is a good crop of **lettuce**, start using the first plants when small; try not to end up with lots of huge plants at risk of going to seed.

- Early **strawberries** will ripen this month from pots brought into the polytunnel earlier in the year. Pick as the fruit ripens and keep an eye out for mildew, removing any affected fruit.

- Keep picking **courgettes** while they are small and still a treat. Check under leaves for lurking marrows – these may inhibit new fruit from growing.

- **Mangetout peas** and **broad beans** will still be cropping abundantly under cover. Evict these at the end of the month if outdoor ones are producing well, and especially if you need the space for other crops.

- Baby **carrots** and early **potatoes** can be harvested now from early sowings. These may be small, but oh so delicious! If growing potatoes in buckets, simply slip a hand down the side and remove a few roots while leaving the plant to grow more. Carrots aren't so easy to remove: turn the pot upside down and shake it hard.

- Pick the last of the **spring cabbage** before summer catches up. If this crop is taking up too much space, plant sweetcorn or tomatoes in gaps in between. Space will be freed up when the cabbage is removed.

JUNE

Things can get very hot in the June polytunnel. The cold nights are gone (in all except an extraordinary year) and tender plants start growing with a vengeance. Plants need to make a heavy crop in the next few months and you need to do everything possible to encourage strong, steady growth. Young tomatoes, melons and cucumbers will flourish with the extra heat, provided they are supplied with water and given an occasional feed, and doors are opened to let a warm breeze drift through.

Weather report

June can be the hottest, sunniest month of the year. It can also be the driest. There is little chance of gales, and daylight hours are long. If high pressure sets in it can stay for weeks, but in some years the heat can be late to arrive and in others a cold wet airflow seems to persist. Whatever the weather throws at us, the polytunnel is a sheltered space. This might mean that it gets too hot on bright sunny days, so plan any work for mornings and evenings. On bad days, enjoy the shelter and work in the polytunnel at any time of the day.

June jobs in brief

Water carefully and ventilate to create a healthy growing environment
Mulch to keep moisture in the ground
Make a few sowings
Mist tomatoes and nip out side shoots
Plant out melons, peppers and aubergines

OPPOSITE TOP: Pick ripe strawberries
OPPOSITE BOTTOM: First courgettes
LEFT: June polytunnel

Grow summer lettuce in the shade of tall plants

Pollinate melons
Thin grapes
Tie large plants into supports
Remove any diseased foliage
Feed growing plants, especially in pots and growbags
Pick lots of early summer crops
Watch out for pests and diseases

Time to sow
Lettuce
Salad leaves
Sweetcorn
Spinach
Florence fennel
Cucumber
Kohl rabi
Parsley
French beans
Broccoli
Kale
Beetroot

Thoughts on June sowings
- Although the polytunnel should be bursting with lush summer growth, now is the time to start thinking about autumn and winter crops. Most sowings for these can be made in July and August and it isn't essential to sow in June. However, it makes sense to locate seed of **spring cabbage, Swiss chard, kohl rabi, winter lettuce, pak choi, Florence fennel, mizuna, mibuna, corn salad, oriental greens**, etc., so that they are all ready to sow next month. And there are still some seeds you can start this month in order to keep one step ahead.
- **Lettuce** and **salad leaves** should be sown every four weeks throughout the summer to give a constant supply.

☑ If you want to grow successful lettuces in a polytunnel through the summer months, grow them in the shade created by tall-growing plants.

- Try sowing **sweetcorn** in June rather than miss out on the crop. In a poor summer these plants may not reach best expectations, but in an Indian summer they can achieve a reasonable harvest of full cobs. Sow two seeds per station, directly into the border. Sow in blocks, allowing 30cm/12in between each sowing point. Remove the weakest seedling to allow the strongest one in each couple to grow on. This gives late sowings the best chance.
- **Florence fennel**, sown at the end of the month, will grow a healthy crop for late autumn and early winter. Sow seed thinly in deep pots or trays.
- **Cucumbers** *can* be sown in early June. These will grow fast to give a late crop.

If this is the only option, it is worth a try.

- Many **overwintered brassicas** do really well under cover: they give earlier and cleaner crops than those grown outside. The problem is that the polytunnel is usually bursting at the seams with summer crops and no one is going to make space for slow-growing winter greens. These can be sown later than greens for outdoor crops (June sowings of **sprouting broccoli** and **kale** can be very successful), but an alternative is to buy in a few plants and keep these in large pots outside the tunnel door. These can go into the polytunnel when space clears. These plants may seem smaller than ones from the same sowing that are planted in an outdoor bed, but don't worry. They will soon catch up and overtake outdoor plants, and will even crop a few weeks earlier.

- If there is space in the polytunnel, it is worth making a second sowing of **dwarf French beans** in June. These can be sown directly into the ground in a double row (rows 20cm/8in apart with 15cm/6in between plants), or in pots to be planted out in a few weeks' time. June sowings can crop really well, even in a poor summer, and should give good pickings into the autumn.

- **Climbing French beans** can still be sown at the beginning of June. Sow *in situ*, 20cm/8in apart in a trench filled with moisture-retaining compost. Beans like plenty of water, so anything that will help keep moisture in the soil is a bonus.

- **Basil** can still be sown in early June, but it is much better to buy a pot of young plants from the supermarket (look in the fruit and veg section). Choose short, strong plants and split these into large pots in clumps of three or four. Soak the root ball before planting.

Dwarf French beans

- Sow **kohl rabi** in late June for autumn crops. Sow thinly in pots and transplant out as space clears. This crop can even be dotted around among others if space is tight.

- **Beetroot** can be started in cells for a winter crop. Seedlings won't take any harm from being transplanted in a few weeks' time.

Tomatoes: flowers, fruit and side shoots

Spray early tomato flowers with a mist of water to ensure the first fruit set. This isn't necessary with later flowers, but those in early June will certainly benefit. Larger tomatoes will usually flower a few weeks behind the cherry ones and beefsteak varieties may only start flowering in June. The lower trusses of cherry varieties should be filling up with green fruit and there may even be some ripe tomatoes before the month is out.

Fruit starts to set from the top of a tomato truss

☑ Ripening at this point in the year depends on sunshine levels, but once some tomatoes ripen, they will give off a gas to stimulate other fruit close by to do the same. For this reason I never strip all red fruit off the first ripening truss.

If lower leaves overshadow trusses, remove a few to allow light in. There should be plenty of leaves growing further up the stem to feed the plant.

Keep removing
side shoots

Keep nipping side shoots out of the joints between leaf and stem on all except bush tomatoes. If left to grow, the plant will put more energy into growing leaf and shoot than into fruit. Side shoots spring up from around the base of the plant as well as where the leaves meet the stem. Check, check and check again – it's amazing how more always seem to appear.

☑ If the main shoot is damaged or weakened in any way, you can grow a strong side shoot on as a replacement and nip the main shoot out.

Tomatoes: support, water and feed

Tomato plants grow tall and need plenty of support, so remember to tie the main stem in to a pole, cane or string. Ties every 15–20cm/6–8in do a good job. If using thin string, wind it around a few times, so that it doesn't cut or break the stem. Always allow enough slack for the stem to thicken as the plant grows.

Correct watering can be the key to productive plants. The aim is to encourage roots to go as deep as possible and hence plants will be more able to survive through the summer months. Water tomato plants really thoroughly every couple of days, soaking the soil well. Tomatoes need lots of water, but they hate sitting in soggy soil day after day. Wait until the soil's surface has dried out before watering again. It is best to water in the evening or early morning, as this gives a chance for moisture to soak down into the soil and less is lost through evaporation. Tomatoes in pots and growbags will need a good soaking every day. This may even need to be done twice a day in really hot weather. Tap the side of a pot with a stick if unsure: pots sound hollow when the compost is dry.

One red
tomato helps
others to ripen

Tomato plants always benefit from a potash-rich liquid feed. Many tomato feeds are based on seaweed. Either buy in a concentrated organic one or make a brew (see Part 7). Both should be diluted before use. For the non-squeamish, urine makes an excellent liquid feed for tomatoes. Dilute the contents of the chamber pot with twice the amount of water before pouring around plants. Apply a feed every seven to ten days while fruit is swelling. Feed plants in containers every seven days. Diluted liquid feeds can be poured into the bottle watering system (see page 24), or over the surface of the soil.

☑ For a 'quick hit' spray the leaves with a fine mist of seaweed feed. Take care: nozzles will block and sprayers won't work if there are any lumps of organic material floating in the liquid feed. If necessary, flick the liquid over the leaves with a soft brush.

Tomatoes: disease

Watch out for signs of disease (see Part 5) and remove any affected leaves, or squash pests before the problem spreads.
• Moulds, mineral shortage and virus disease can discolour leaves and stems.
• Whitefly might take up residence on the lower sides of tomato leaves.

- Blight can strike in June, although tomatoes grown under cover can be kept free from spores by keeping doors closed on the dull, humid days that favour the spread of this disease.

Cucumbers

Plants sown in early March should be cropping abundantly. A healthy cucumber plant can produce between twenty and fifty fruits in a season. Some fruits may be less than perfect in appearance, but they will taste just as good. Keep picking to ensure that more grow. Plants should have fruits at all stages of development at any one time. If large cucumbers are left to mature and ripen seed, the plant will think it has achieved its mission and will stop producing young fruit.

If the variety isn't an all-female one, check to see if male flowers should be nipped out. This prevents pollination of female flowers and hence avoids the problem of bitter fruit. Recheck the seed packet: it will tell you if nipping is needed or not.

Keep twirling stems around strings, or tying them in to sticks, to provide support. Once the stem reaches the roof, let it trail back down again, but make sure that the stem doesn't make too acute a turn, as otherwise it might snap at the highest point.

Cucumbers need careful watering. In fact, they do best with that peculiar mix of a free-draining yet damp root run. Make sure the compost is damp, but never too wet. This may mean watering twice a day to keep up with the demands of these thirsty plants. Give cucumbers a spray over the leaves – they enjoy a humid climate and may find the polytunnel too dry at times.

Cucumbers do well if fresh compost is piled up around the lower parts of the stem. Do this every couple of weeks. New roots will soon grow from the buried part of the stem. This helps overcome problems with root rot.

One cucumber plant can provide lots of fruit

Other cucumber problems

Add a teaspoonful of Epsom salts to the watering can if leaves show signs of magnesium deficiency – older leaves turning yellow between dark green veins.

If the soil is too dry, powdery mildew might show as white splashes of mould on the leaves. Alter the watering regime and use a milk spray to combat this disease. Red spider mite can be a problem in dry conditions; to avoid it, keep foliage damp.

For more on pests and diseases, see Part 5.

NOTE: Cucumbers are sensitive plants and you may do more harm than good by using a bug spray. Even ones based on derris or pyrethrum can do harm.

Peppers, aubergines and melons: planting out

These are some of the most tender crops and little is lost by waiting until early June to plant them out. In fact, all these will suffer if they are put out in an unheated structure where night-time temperatures drop below 12°C/54°F. Choose plants with strong stems and plenty of leaf. If leaves are curled they might have greenfly hiding in the folds.

Pepper flower

Peppers

Slow and steady growth is the aim (for soil and planting techniques, see May). Tall plants will need support, so provide stakes and tie in stems. This will help the plants support a heavy crop. First flowers should appear in June. These will be self-fertile and won't need much help with pollination, but to ensure an early set, lightly mist with tepid water and tap the flowering stems gently. Peppers need plenty of water. The flowers tend to drop off if roots are dry, or if humidity is low.

Aubergines

It may still be necessary to cover young aubergine plants with an extra covering. This can provide an essential bit of extra warmth. Ideally, aubergines should be kept away from draughts, so don't plant them near the polytunnel door.

☑ I use a propagator frame (once it has finished the job of raising small plants) as a large cloche to cover aubergine plants.

Pollinating an aubergine flower

Aubergine plants will start to produce lovely purple flowers towards the middle of the month. These may need a hand with pollination. Transfer pollen with a soft paintbrush. Dampen the bristles by running the brush across your tongue – no more, as it will be too wet. Successfully pollinated flowers set marble-sized fruit behind the petals. If petals stick to this, peel them off. If flowers aren't successfully pollinated they shrivel and drop off the plant. Don't worry if this happens – more flowers will grow – but the best fruit is often grown from the earliest set.

Aubergines need careful watering. If the weather is dull and damp, don't spray any water over the leaves. However, in a hot dry spell it is essential to spray the leaves in order to ensure fruit set. Spraying with water will also help to keep red spider mite under control. Aubergines are particularly susceptible to this pest.

Debate on aubergines

Some people advocate nipping out the tops of aubergine plants when they reach 20cm/8in high. This forces them to produce a more bushy plant. I never do this and I'll tell you why. It's hard enough to get a good crop of aubergines in an average summer. In a bad summer it can be almost impossible. Anything that defers the crop (even though it might mean you get more fruit in a good, long, hot summer) can mean a delay to first fruits. Where I live, quite high above sea level, the first flowers are the ones most likely to make successful fruit. If I delay first flowers, I might get more of them, but too late to produce good aubergines. If you live in a warmer area, however, try nipping the top of one plant and see how it does. It may be that the technique suits you better than it suits me.

Melons

March-sown plants can open the first flowers by the end of May or early June. Female flowers have small melon-shaped swellings behind them, whereas males are borne on a thin straight stem. The female flowers won't set fruit unless they are fertilized. Break off a male flower and introduce pollen manually to make sure this happens. The usual advice is to wait until there are four female flowers open on the same day, pulling off single flowers before that, to ensure that four melons grow on each plant rather than one singleton. This is all well and good, but don't wait weeks for the hallowed day and leave the whole thing too late – two or three melons are better than none!

Twist melon stems around support strings

Melons can be left to ramble over the ground, but this is really a waste of space when they are growing in a small polytunnel. Use strings tied in to the framework to support growing plants. Simply twirl the growing stems around the string; tendrils will then twist around to provide a firmer grip. Growth can be very rapid at this time of year, so don't leave lengths of unsupported stem to flop and break.

Melons do particularly well in growbags, but it is always worth making a few drainage holes in the bottom and sitting the bag on a layer of compost to facilitate wandering roots.

Sweetcorn

If you put plants in the ground last month, stems can be 60cm/24in tall in June. Sweetcorn is a really greedy plant. If growth starts to slow, give it a liquid feed; otherwise let plants reach for the sky on the stock of nutrients dug in at planting time. Water regularly to optimize the number of cobs per stalk.

Sweetcorn should be planted 30cm/12in apart in blocks to aid pollination (for planting techniques, see May).

☑ Some sweetcorn varieties mustn't be allowed to cross-pollinate with other varieties. This is especially true of the supersweet varieties, which will lose some of their sweetness. However, I have successfully grown two varieties at opposite ends of a 10m/33ft polytunnel without any obvious loss of taste. Without wind to carry the pollen, most of this will fall close to where it was produced.

French beans

If you sowed beans in pots last month, plant them out now (for planting technique, see April and May). Think about where to position climbing beans, as they can form an effective curtain that restricts sunlight to anything it overshadows. This can be a bonus for salad crops, which don't fare so well in the full summer glare. Alternatively, grow climbing beans on a north wall, or in a north–south alignment so that all sides get some sun.

March- and April-sown dwarf beans should be cropping well in June. Pick the pods when small and the plants will continue to produce bountiful crops for several weeks. Remember that all legumes need plenty of water when they are in flower. Make sure water isn't just shed by the leaves: get the hose underneath to make sure soil is wet around the roots.

Climbing French varieties grow rapidly and will twine around a support string once they have found it. Just give a nudge in the right direction when the young shoots first start to seek a support.

Red spider mite loves French beans and can get out of control in a dry environment (see Part 5). Leaves turn a reddish brown colour and small mites can often be seen on the underside. Spray water over and under leaves to reduce the severity of the attack.

Grape vines

Check over established grape vines. There should be small bunches of embryo fruit at the beginning of June. By the end of the month this will have started to swell. If you haven't mulched the vine with manure, use a nitrogen-rich liquid feed around the roots – anything to get nutrients to the growing crop. Remember to water around the base of the vine. If this is planted outdoors and trained round to grow into the tunnel, it can be easy to forget to water in dry weather, but it is essential to do so if your aim is to grow a good crop of grapes.

Pruning a grape vine

Pruning grape vines

There is an art to producing an immaculate vine full of perfect fruit, but don't get so intimidated about pruning that you avoid the task altogether. The vine may not look so amazing as one that is perfectly cropped and trained, but a basic pruning job will still lead to plenty of grapes.

1. Any lateral shoot that has formed two embryo bunches should be stopped by cutting out the growing point. Cut this after the first or second leaf beyond the fruit. Choose whether to cut after one or two leaves on the basis of how much shade the vine casts.
2. Stop non-fruiting lateral shoots after they have grown two or three leaves.
3. Don't prune the main stem, but do tie it in and support any new growth, so that the vine doesn't break under the weight of a heavy crop.

Pruning new vines

Leave two main shoots to grow on and cut side shoots after they have grown five leaves. Choose the strongest of the two as a leader next year. Pick off any bunches of embryo fruit that form in the first year.

Picking basil

Basil

This glorious herb will be ready for picking at just about the time tomatoes start to ripen – a perfect taste combination! Pinch out the top cluster of leaves on each shoot before a flower spike appears. New clusters will grow from the small leaves lower down the stem. Nip off any flower spikes that start to grow. Flowering affects the flavour of the leaves, so nip the tops regularly to keep basil at its best.

Strawberries
Plants will still be cropping well in their pots in the polytunnel. Keep them watered and fed while fruits are swelling. Harvest ripe fruits before slugs or birds eat them and remove any fruit that shows signs of grey mould (see Part 5). Move pots out of the tunnel as soon as they stop being productive, to make room for other plants.

☑ Put a stick in the pots that have the most productive plants. These are the ones you will want to use to propagate new plants for next year. Once you have picked the berries it can be hard to remember which plants cropped best.

Plenty of strawberries

Holiday time?
June can be a relatively easy month in the polytunnel. Admittedly, there are growing plants that need ongoing care and attention, but most of these will be planted out and growing well. The autumn and winter sowings don't need to be made for another few weeks. In fact, if you are planning a summer holiday, the end of June is about as good as it gets in terms of not leaving too much responsibility for seedlings, or excessive harvesting duties, in other hands.

☑ If you are going away, sink pots of seedlings into the border soil. You can lift these when you return, but in the meantime the roots will keep at a more even temperature.

Ventilation and watering
Fine-tune ventilation by opening one door or two, depending on the day. Remember that you can prop doors so that they stay just ajar, or fling them fully open to catch any puff of air. Of course, if it is cold and wet, doors should still be closed at night to keep in any warmth. Avoid hot and humid conditions, which favour the spread of disease.

Water regularly and don't let anything dry out completely. Spray overhead to reduce problems with red spider mite and dampen paths to keep humidity up. Remember that cucumbers prefer a higher humidity and will always benefit from a spray of water over the leaves. Tomatoes and aubergines like their leaves to be a little drier, but try to wet the soil thoroughly around the roots every couple of days. Pay special attention to the needs of growbags and containers.

Mulch
Always wet the soil well before covering it with mulch. Lots of readily available materials can be used to cover the ground: black polythene, cardboard, grass clippings, cocoa shell, bark chips, mulch matting, cut comfrey leaves, etc. Admittedly, there are problems with some of these: polythene can make a good hiding place for slugs; comfrey rots down rapidly and so doesn't cover the soil for long, although it does provide tomatoes with potash; and grass clippings must be free from seeds. However, if water is in short supply, it's wise to look at mulch as a way of reducing evaporation.

☑ Mulch is particularly useful if you are going away on holiday, as it can reduce the number of errors that an enthusiastic neighbour might bring to bear.

Enjoy the June harvest

Courgettes

Cucumbers

Tomatoes

French beans

Salad leaves

Lettuce

Basil

Kohl rabi

Potatoes

Carrots

Mangetout peas

Broad beans

Some harvesting hints

- There should be plenty of tasty treats this month. As usual the key is to keep harvesting in order to keep plants producing. Eat things while they are small! That's the joy of June. The freshest tastiest crops are pouring in. There will be plenty more to follow, so leave nothing to grow too large and tough.
- There should be lots of **salad leaves**. These can, of course, grow outdoors, but the polytunnel ones come faster and are more likely to be blemish free.
- **Cucumbers, kohl rabi,** fingerling **carrots,** tiny **courgettes,** slim **French beans, strawberries** and the first **cherry tomatoes, basil** for pesto . . . Summer has certainly arrived and the picking is easy as can be!

Lots to harvest
in June

JULY

The polytunnel can feel a bit like a jungle in July. All those plants that seemed so widely spaced in May are jostling for room and the air can be hot and humid. It's important to ensure that light and fresh air can reach where they are needed. Keep bulky foliage trimmed and leave doors open so that plants can avail themselves of any cooling breeze. If the weather is hot, try to work under cover in the mornings and evenings, and water at those times too. Spray overhead to cool down any plants that don't like too much heat and damp down paths to keep air moist.

Weather report

It would be nice to say that July is a glorious month. Indeed it can be lovely, and it can produce beautiful sunny days that record some of the highest temperatures, but July can also live up to its reputation for being the wettest month of the summer. If a series of wet south-westerly depressions sets in, all except the most eastern counties will see a lot of rain. Weather patterns such as this tend to persist once they become established. But it's not all doom and gloom! High pressure can persist too, so at least part of the month might bring a heat wave.

The July jungle

Start sowing for autumn and winter crops

July jobs in brief
Patrol the polytunnel every day
Start sowing for autumn and winter crops
Leave doors open
Keep borders free of weeds
Water regularly, damp paths and mist overhead on hot days
Apply liquid feeds
Give a hand with pollination
Peg down strawberry runners
Keep harvesting
Control pests and diseases

Time to sow

Spring cabbage	Dwarf French beans
Swiss chard	Broccoli
Spinach/spinach beet	Rocket
Pak choi	Winter purslane
Kale	Mizuna
Beetroot	Mibuna
Fennel	Lamb's lettuce
Kohl rabi	Land cress
Winter lettuce	Turnip
Oriental leaves	Potatoes
Parsley	

Thoughts on July sowings

• The real test for a polytunnel gardener isn't how many tomatoes can be grown in a good summer but how full the space is through the autumn, winter and early spring. An unheated polytunnel can be used to grow a wide variety of vegetables through the coldest months of the year, but only if you make sowings (or buy in plug plants) during the summer months.

☑ If you intend to go on holiday in July, and don't have an enthusiastic garden-minder near by, leave sowings until August. You might get slower autumn crops, but at least seedlings won't die for want of water while you are away.

• The first sowing of **spinach, spring cabbage** and a wide range of winter **salad leaves** can be made in pots or in drills in July. Sow summer varieties of **lettuce** for autumn crops, but also make the first sowings of winter varieties. Some favourites are 'Winter Density', 'Winter Gem' and 'Lattughino'. 'Valdor' and 'All the Year Round' give softer leaves, but both grow well in a winter polytunnel.
• Ignore the seed packets and try sowing **Florence fennel, beetroot** and even **broccoli**. All these give great winter and early spring harvests in a polytunnel.
• **Swiss chard** – 'Bright Lights' or 'Ruby' varieties – provides vibrant-coloured stems and tasty leaves. This crop comes into its own in the New Year, when it is good to have colour in a winter vegetable.

- **Dwarf French beans** sown now will crop through October, or even into November. Sow all these in deep pots and keep them on a bench, near an open door if it is hot.
- Sow **parsley** in a pot to prick out and transplant later. This sowing will provide pickings right through the winter.
- Try making a sowing of **potatoes** in containers. These can be started outdoors, but bring them into the polytunnel as soon as foliage pokes through. This reduces the likelihood of blight attack.

☑ Try using sprouted potato tubers left over from a spring planting. These may look shrivelled, but if sprouts are healthy, they can still grow on with surprising vigour once they get their roots into some good compost. Always use a blight-resistant variety like 'Sarpo Mira' – this avoids problems with late blight.

The daily patrol

A lot of work in the July polytunnel is based on the philosophy of 'Take a good look round and see what needs to be done.' It's all too easy to focus on one particular job, while not noticing that something else is crying out for attention. Watering can take up a lot of time, but it is possible to use this time to turn a leaf and look for pests, to see if a cucumber is ready for picking, to scatter pollen over sweetcorn or to check for unwanted shoots at the base of tomato plants. Work around the tunnel and take a quick look at each thing. Try to do this regularly: it shouldn't take long and should be an enjoyable task. This way you can spot potential problems before they develop into serious ones.

Ventilation is vital in the summer months

Ventilation

You can avoid a lot of problems if you maintain good ventilation throughout the summer months. Moulds proliferate in a stuffy, hot, humid environment and once plants wilt, it is hard to get them back to their former glory. If the sun is up long before you are, it might be wise to leave doors open overnight. If necessary, hang fine-mesh netting across open doors: this will reduce wind chill but still allow some movement of air.

Weeding

Plants tend to be a bit overcrowded in a polytunnel and the last thing they need is competition from weeds. Take weeding seriously and it will become less of a chore. If you remove weeds when they are small, and before they seed or spread, numbers will gradually decrease. It's easy to keep a polytunnel free of weeds. A hoe works fine among widely spaced plants, but do be careful not to damage shallow roots, or put holes in the polythene. Hand weeding isn't a chore if done regularly. It takes only a short while to work systematically around the beds and pots.

NOTE: Some people swear that leaving the beds covered with weeds helps keep moisture in the soil. This may be true, and it might seem an easy way to operate for a start, but weed problems only get worse if they are left to grow out of control and there will be nothing easy about the resultant mess. Mulch will do a much better job of keeping moisture in the soil without competing for water and nutrients.

A water reservoir for a tomato plant

Watering technique

Careful watering is essential during the summer months. Plants kept on short water rations will never grow well and in order to survive they will attempt to set seed. It's always best to water in the evening (or early morning) rather than during the heat of the day. This allows water to soak down into the soil and reduces the amount lost through evaporation. If water restrictions are in place, use water barrels to collect rainwater.

If water is in short supply, try to be economical in its use. Wet around the root area of plants and where nothing is planted leave dry soil. Never flood water on to the top of a mound of soil only to watch it roll away down the sides. Instead make a depression to retain water and pour slowly and steadily, allowing one lot to soak in before adding more. Mulch will always be of benefit, as it keeps moisture in the soil where it is needed.

Plants in pots and containers may need daily watering, although you can avoid having to do this if you stand pots in a tray of water. Plants such as cucumbers and melons should be lightly watered round the base of the stem on a daily basis and sprayed overhead at the same time. Repeat this action several times on hot days and damp down any paths as well. Try to get a balance between the humid conditions preferred by cucumbers and aubergines and the slightly drier air conditions preferred by tomatoes and peppers.

Cucumbers

Keep harvesting regularly. There should be bumper crops of cucumbers now. Remove any small, discoloured fruit that doesn't look as if it will develop. This allows new fruit to set further up the stem. Always pick ripe cucumbers, even if there are too many to eat; if ripe fruits are left unpicked, the plant will stop producing. Give surplus cucumbers away, make pickles or at worst throw them on the compost heap.

Remember to keep adding an extra layer of compost around the base of the stem to maintain healthy root growth.

Cucumbers like a moist atmosphere and they will be more prone to disease, or attack by red spider mite, if grown in a dry environment. Watch out for powdery mildew, which appears as white dots on leaves. The dots can spread until a whole leaf is covered (see Part 5).

Sweetcorn

These really are thirsty plants, so don't stint on water. Use a hosepipe, if possible, to deliver moisture right to the base of each plant.

Tall stems will grow to above head height and they may end up squashed against the polythene. As long as pollen can still fall freely, this isn't a problem. Male tassels thrust up from the top of the stem. Pollen drops down from the tassels on to the silks that protrude from the female cobs, which grow in the joint between leaf and stem. Some plants will produce only one cob, others will form two and, in a good summer, a few plants might go as far as three. Good pollination is the key to large, full cobs. In outdoor conditions the wind helps spread pollen, but in the polytunnel it is best to give a helping hand. Shake a few stems in each block of plants to release a shower of pollen. Do this every day until all the cobs are swelling nicely. Incomplete pollination leads to poorly filled cobs. Be gentle: don't shake too hard, as the stems might break.

If growing more than one variety, try to confine pollen spread to like with like. This can be difficult, but some varieties don't fill cobs well if they cross-pollinate.

Silks on the end of sweetcorn cobs

☑ Take care when weeding between sweetcorn plants. The stems are brittle and will snap if bent.

Pumpkins and squash

These grow rapidly and there should be plenty of male and female flowers this month. Pollination of the first flowers can be slow if they are left to their own devices. The best solution is to pick a male flower and strip back the petals, leaving a pollen-laden spike. Pollen can then be introduced directly to female flowers (these have a small pumpkin shape behind them).

If pumpkin foliage is getting out of hand, trim off leaves, or train stems to creep out of an open door.

☑ The beauty of growing pumpkins in a polytunnel is that pollen is early enough, and stays dry enough, to use to set the first fruit. If outdoor pumpkins aren't pollinating well, simply take a male flower spike from a plant grown in the tunnel and use this to pollinate outdoor flowers.

Pollinating a pumpkin

Basil

Basil will be at its best through July and August. The leaves need to be picked regularly to ensure that more are produced. Nip out any flower spikes, as flowering can make the leaves taste bitter. Harvest carefully so that the plants continue to crop. Pick the whole top cluster of leaves from the end of a shoot; this allows the small shoots that are just appearing in lower joints to grow new clusters. Never strip a plant and don't pick the lower, large leaves, as these will help to feed the plant for many weeks yet.

Tomatoes

Sun-ripened tomatoes come into their own in July. The earliest are the cherry varieties such as 'Sungold', which has orange fruit and must be the sweetest variety going. Fruit at the top of the truss will ripen first. This ripe fruit gives off a gas that speeds up the ripening of fruit lower down the truss. Wait until lower fruit starts to colour slightly, and then pick the ripe fruit from the top.

Harvesting tomatoes

French bean flowers

Low-hanging, long trusses may trail on the ground and fruit can be susceptible to slug damage. If this is a problem, raise them off the ground with twiggy sticks.

Beefsteak varieties are always slower to ripen than cherry ones. Don't be impatient: these giants of the tomato world will colour up nicely next month. If tomatoes are slow to ripen in a dull year, place a banana or one or two red tomatoes among the green trusses. These will help kick-start the ripening process.

If border soil dries out rapidly, it is worth using a mulch. Using a mulch of comfrey is a great way to provide tomatoes with potash, but mix it with something like grass clippings to give better coverage over bare soil.

Remember to keep feeding with liquid feeds, such as seaweed, every seven to ten days. Once plants have set four trusses, give them a nitrogen-rich feed. This stops plants running thin at the top, helps sustain the growth of many more trusses and ensures that cropping will continue into the autumn.

Keep nipping out side shoots and start removing lower leaves if they are discoloured, badly curled or overshadowing ripening trusses. New shoots will still sprout from the base of the stem. Nip these out in the same way as side shoots, as they draw the energy of the plant away from fruit production.

Tomatoes and blight

Keep an eye out for signs of disease (see Part 5). In a damp July, blight will rear its head and it can find its way under cover to blacken tomato leaves. The disease will spread to discolour fruit, but there are a few things that you can do to hold it at bay:

- Keep doors shut, if possible, on damp misty days that favour the spread of blight. Physically excluding spores from the polytunnel is obviously ideal, but don't risk sweltering crops if temperatures rise too high.
- Remove any blackened or discoloured leaves. These may be a sign of blight or another disease, and it is best to get them out of the way before the problem spreads.
- If blight is a regular problem, grow a blight-resistant variety such as 'Ferline'.

Climbing French beans

April sowings will start to crop in July. Harvest regularly while the beans are small. Plants need plenty of water to supply such rapid growth, so don't let the soil dry out; if it does, plants will become more at risk from attack by red spider mite (see Part 5).

Aubergines

Keep pollinating flowers with a soft paintbrush until four or five fruits are set per plant. Peel away any petals that stick to small fruit: these can be a starting point for grey mould to take hold. Early varieties might start cropping by the end of July.

If plants are in a growbag, remember to start using a liquid feed; the nutrients in the growbag will be exhausted after six to eight weeks of growth. Feed every ten days while fruit is swelling.

Slugs might nibble at growing fruit. This isn't too much of a problem, since aubergines seem to heal small wounds as they grow; just stop the pests before they make large holes.

Peppers

Plants should be covered in small white flowers. The flowers are self-fertile, although, as mentioned last month, it is worth tapping branches and misting with water if the air is dry. Flowering continues even as fruit starts to swell. This can ensure a long cropping period, with fruit through to the winter.

Sturdy well-grown plants should carry a crop of small peppers by the end of the month. There is no need to limit the number of fruit per plant and some can comfortably produce twenty to thirty peppers over the next few months. Use a liquid feed every week while fruit is swelling. Peppers are part of the same family as tomatoes and they like the same type of feed: high potash but not excessive nitrogen (seaweed is ideal).

Watch out for slugs eating into the heart of developing fruit – peppers will rot if damaged in this way. A few ferric phosphate pellets will stop the problem in an organically approved way.

NOTE: Green peppers are unripe versions of red ones. Pick them green if that's your preference, or leave them to ripen and change colour on the plant.

☑ Peppers like hot sunny weather. If the month is dull, lay aluminium foil on the ground between plants. This reflects more sunlight on to the plants and helps fruit to ripen; it also keeps the roots warm. But you must remember to water underneath the foil. The same trick can be applied to aubergines.

Melons

Keep pollinating flowers if fruit hasn't set and twine the stems up strings to keep fruit off the ground. 'Sweetheart' melons that set fruit early in June will be ready for eating in July. Fruit should be around 10cm/4in in diameter and should 'give' a little if pressed. Ripe melons can smell delectably sweet. If in doubt, leave fruit to ripen for a day or two longer, but never until it rots or falls from the vine.

Larger fruiting varieties will take a few weeks longer to reach maturity. Use nets (the ones from bags of oranges are ideal) to support individual melons, so that the weight doesn't break stems. Tie the nets on to the framework of the polytunnel or support canes.

Grapes

Vines are thirsty plants. They shouldn't really be rooted inside the polytunnel, but if they are, water daily so to make sure that both the vine

Small fruit and flowers on an aubergine plant

Immature fruit on a melon plant

Swelling grapes

BELOW: Peg
down strawberry
runners
OPPOSITE TOP:
Delicious vine
tomatoes
OPPOSITE
BOTTOM: A ripe
corn cob

and nearby plants have enough moisture. If the vine is trained in from outside the tunnel, the roots will need watering in dry weather.

A grape vine can produce a huge number of bunches in a good year. Be brave and remove small and semi-formed bunches (up to half may have to go) so that the remaining ones grow well. Keep removing leaves and prune back side shoots to allow light and air through to the grapes.

Also, it is worth thinning out the smallest grapes from a bunch. Use a pair of small pointed scissors to reach into the bunch and nip out individual stems. This allows the larger grapes to grow well and form a decent bunch. If all the grapes are left to grow on, some will stay small and the bunch can become so tightly packed that few of the grapes will reach their full potential. Thinning is a time-consuming job. Look on it as a meditation: dwell on the fruit that is to come and it may not seem so bad!

NOTE: Thinning individual grapes is a fiddly process, so only bother to do this for dessert varieties. Grapes for wine making don't need to be thinned in this way.

Strawberries

Plants in pots will finish cropping in June or early July. Move them out of the polytunnel, but keep them within the sphere of care. Strawberries produce runners when they finish fruiting and these should be pegged down into small pots. Take runners from the best plants rather than the worst producers, and all should bode well for the next year's supply. Take only the first plant on each runner – although some will produce two or more, the later ones will be weaker. Once the runner has rooted into a pot of its own, it can be severed from the parent plant.

☑ Although some people say you should discard the parent plant and grow on only the young ones, I always keep the good producers for another year (or even two). If you put sticks in to mark them while fruiting, they should be easy enough to identify. Give the plants a haircut, removing all discoloured leaves and debris from the pot and leaving only the smallest leaves untouched. Two- and three year-old plants in pots can go on to produce superb crops.

Courgettes

Keep picking courgettes for as long as you need them. If you have plenty of these cropping outdoors, it might be time to think about evicting the ones in the polytunnel. If space is in short supply, this might be an essential act. However, if you can spare the space, it's worth leaving one or two courgette plants to grow on inside the polytunnel. In a bad summer outdoor crops might fail, but the covered ones will guarantee fruit all summer long. In a good summer, polytunnel courgettes might just add to the glut, but they will continue cropping into the autumn long after the outdoor ones are done.

Powdery mildew shows as a white dusting over leaves and is directly connected to overcrowding and dry soil.

Enjoy the July harvest

Tomatoes	Basil
Cucumbers	Melons
Courgettes	Strawberries
French beans	Sweetcorn
Salad a-plenty	Spinach

Some harvesting hints

- The kitchen should be full of produce from the polytunnel. **Melons** might grace the fruit bowl, along with last **strawberries**.
- **Cucumbers**, **courgettes** and **salad** can roll in with alarming regularity and it's hard to keep up with the **tomato** supply. Don't be a martyr to excessive production: evict a **cucumber** plant if there are six of the beasts looking really healthy and producing fresh fruit each day.
- Just a dozen March-sown **French bean** plants can be producing enough beans to feed a family. Look under the leaves for hidden beans.
- **Sweetcorn** cobs might start to mature at the end of July. Pick these while young and sweet for some of the tastiest treats.
- Always pick, pick, pick, as this keeps most plants producing. Non-productive plants have no place in this exceptional growing environment.

AUGUST

August brings baskets of tomatoes, fresh-picked corn cobs, cucumbers, peppers, melons, aubergines and much more besides. Enjoy it all! This is a time to appreciate what a wonderful space the polytunnel is. Even if it's hard to know what to do with all the produce, keep picking so that plants keep producing. Get out the preserving and freezing books or give the surplus away to friends. It shouldn't be hard to find a stand-in gardener for August holidays – all those tasty pickings soon repay for a bit of watering.

Weather report

How we always long for a glorious August! Maybe, just maybe, an anticyclone will persist and keep temperatures high. But a wet July can lead to a wetter August. On top of that, the days are shortening and real sunshine can be in short supply. Have faith! This month often seems to turn itself round: a bad start to the month can improve to give bright sun and clear skies.

Some people consider August the first month of autumn. It can certainly feel that way for northern gardens. Night temperatures can start to dip and heavy dews in the morning might mimic a frost, even though the real thing shouldn't happen for a while yet.

August polytunnel

August jobs in brief

Pot on seedlings until ready to plant out

Keep sowing for winter crops

Feed ripening crops

Check for ripe sweetcorn cobs

Keep foliage away from the polythene

Damp down paths and spray overhead to bring temperatures down

Ventilate continuously

Harvest regularly

Use the glut

Watch out for pests and diseases

Enjoy what you have achieved!

TOP: Keep sowing salad leaves
BOTTOM: Pak choi

Time to sow

French beans	Winter purslane
Kohl rabi	Texel greens
Swiss chard	Spring cabbage
Winter lettuce	Pak choi
Spinach	Turnip
Florence fennel	Kale
Rocket	Oriental salad leaves
Mizuna	Potatoes
Mibuna	Calabrese
Lamb's lettuce (corn salad)	Beetroot
Land cress	

August sowing

- If you made lots of winter sowings in July, there may be no need to make many more in August. On the other hand, a second sowing staggers crops so that they don't all become ready at once and also provides some protection if the first sowing fails. It's always worth sowing a few things this month to ensure there are plenty of crops to pick right through the winter and into spring. Start the process early in August if you didn't make sowings last month.
- **French beans** sown early in August can sometimes produce a successful autumn crop, provided there aren't any really low temperatures to contend with.
- Sow 'Snowball' **turnips** and a winter-hardy variety like 'Noir d'Hiver' this month. Sow seed in shallow drills 30cm/12in apart. These will give a good crop of creamy roots in the winter.
- Try sowing **pak choi** in a pot, to plant out and grow on in the polytunnel. This will suffer if there are really low temperatures, but it often provides good pickings up until Christmas.
- Sow **perpetual spinach** now, for a continuous supply through the winter.

- If greens are a favourite, now is the time to make a second sowing of **spring cabbage**. Sow seed in tubs and keep young plants in a holding bed or large container until space is freed up by clearing summer crops. Spring cabbage grown in a polytunnel is always sweeter and less tough than that grown outdoors.
- Winter varieties of **lettuce** do very well from a late August sowing, as do most **salad leaves**. For a few different lettuce varieties, try 'Cassandra', 'Winter Crop' or any hardy variety that catches the eye. Most seed catalogues offer a wide range of salad and oriental leaves. Any of these are worth trying and it can be a way to find a star performer. Maybe some will fail from a late sowing, but you will lose little by risking a small pinch of seed. Cut-and-come-again crops should be sown directly where they are to grow. These do really well in large pots as well as in the ground.
- **Florence fennel** is an excellent winter crop. Sow early in August and, in all except the hardest winter, it should keep growing through until the following spring. Start seeds in deep pots with a bit of warmth. Watch out for earwigs and slugs.

NOTE: A prolonged spell of temperatures below 0°C/32°F will cause fennel leaves to flop. If it is really cold for a long period, then you might lose the whole crop.

- For **beetroot** lovers, it's worth making an early August sowing to grow on in the polytunnel. This will produce a crop of tasty small roots in the winter, or early spring if growth is slow. Either way it will be there when outdoor crops are gone. If space is limited, sow seed in cells and plant out, at 12cm/5in apart, as room clears.

Young kohl rabi plants

Young plants
Some of last month's sowings may be ready for planting out now. Alternatively, move them on into larger pots, while waiting for space to free up. Try not to disturb the roots too much. Use a kitchen fork to free up the root ball if seedlings are stuck in pots. Winter crops need to be got into the ground as soon as space clears, as they need to get plenty of growing done before colder weather rolls in.

Food for growing plants
Apologies for repetition about liquid feeds, but applying them is an important summer task. Plants can crop over many months and they have to be fed well throughout that time. If one batch of feed is used up, make another – it will still be needed next month. There are many good feeds available commercially (preferably choose organic options, such as seaweed-based ones). For home-made brews, see Part 7.
- **Tomatoes** can be fed every seven days while fruit is swelling and ripening.
- **Cucumbers, peppers, aubergines** and **melons** appreciate a feed every ten days while bearing fruit. Any plant that has yellow-tinged leaves is probably short of nitrogen and a liquid feed might provide a quick fix.
- Remember that anything grown in containers or growbags will have a limited supply of nutrients. Most compost will provide enough for about two months' growing (depending on the size of the plant and the container). If leaves start to discolour, apply a liquid feed and add a layer of compost around the plant.

☑ Top dressing is a useful way of feeding large plants in pots. Scrape back and remove any loose compost before applying a new layer. Take care not to damage roots in the process.

Tomatoes

- Beefsteak, cherry and medium varieties should all be dripping with ripe fruit in August. Harvest regularly and always before fruit bursts or falls to the ground.
- Tomato varieties that have short trusses, of six or seven fruit, can be left to ripen so that the whole ripe truss can be picked as one. This looks decorative and can be an advantage if your aim is to sell surplus produce. Don't try ripening the whole of a long truss: the top fruit will become overripe and fall before the lower fruit is red enough.
- Side shoots grow from every angle and it is easy to miss them among the foliage. Keep nipping them out and watch for the ones that grow from the base of the stem. Try to keep on top of things, but don't panic if side shoots start to win the battle – tomato plants will do fine if left to grow at this point, and something can be said for letting fresh new leaves take over the job of old diseased ones. They may create a bit of a jungle, but they will still crop well into the autumn.
- Try to tie tomato stems away from the sides of the polytunnel, so that leaves, flowers and fruit don't get squashed against the polythene.
- Check for caterpillar damage. If there are holes in fruit, look in and around the leaves near by to find the culprits. There probably won't be more than one or two and these can be removed.
- Tie in the stem to provide support and feed every seven days.
- Always remove any diseased and discoloured foliage. Keep removing lower leaves to allow light through to ripening fruit.
- Keep the soil damp, to help your plants produce plenty of blemish-free fruits.

Beefsteak tomatoes

☑ One option is to nip the growing point out after four or five trusses are set, to ensure that all fruit ripens well. I prefer to leave plants to grow on unrestricted. Often they set seven or even eight trusses on cherry varieties. If plants ramble, simply tie them on to the next cane along, or the one after that. It may look a little unruly, but you'll get more fruit. Plants that are stopped finish cropping earlier. I love the possibility of picking the last ripe fruit up to Christmas if the year is kind.

Tomatoes can be frozen whole

What to do with surplus tomatoes?

Get out the recipe books and start cooking, because August can bring fruit by the basketful. Sauces, soups, etc. freeze well, and so do whole tomatoes if there isn't time to do anything else. Tomatoes can be frozen whole on trays and ripe trusses of fruit can go into the freezer straight off the plant. Bag these up once they are frozen and use as needed. They will provide a fresh tomato taste, if used in cooked dishes, and you can make chutneys with frozen fruit when the timing suits.

NOTE: Frozen tomatoes soften when thawed and will not be the same as fresh fruit.

Cucumbers

Stems may well have grown to touch the top of the polytunnel this month. Some people like to cut the tops at this point, but it works well to simply turn them around so that they grow back down. Take care not to break the stem where it turns and the bumper crop of cucumbers should continue. Stems need plenty of support, so keep twirling them around strings or canes. Use string to tie stems in if they start to slide under the weight of the crop.

Cucumbers in growbags need regular feeding and plenty of water to keep these thirsty plants producing. If the growbag compost is depleted, simply punch a few holes through the base, so that the roots can feed off the soil below (lift the bag carefully, if necessary, and then lay it back down over a layer of compost or manure).

If fruit tastes bitter, check the seed packet, as the plant may be a variety that demands the removal of all-male flowers. It's not too late to start doing this, but take care to remove every one, preferably before it opens, and preferably every day.

Watch out for signs of mineral deficiency and use a seaweed foliar spray, in the morning or evening, to give a quick feed. Liquid feeds can be watered round the roots every ten days.

Remember to keep harvesting cucumbers, no matter how many that may be. The plants may have pauses in productivity and they will eventually slow down altogether, but the aim is to keep them fruiting for as long as possible.

Melons

Keep twirling the stems around support strings and use nets to support swelling fruit. Check fruit for ripeness, but don't bruise it by squeezing too hard. Try to get the right balance between watering enough to keep fruit swelling and maintaining a free-draining root run. Earth up around the base of the stem, with fresh compost, to help stimulate new root growth.

Nets supporting melons

Melons will only give bumper crops in a hot summer. In a dull, cold year, plants struggle to put on adequate growth and the fruit that sets may never achieve a decent size. If no fruit has set by August, things might not look too promising. However, if plants are strong and growing well, keep pollinating the flowers, as an Indian summer might see some perfectly respectable fruit in a few weeks' time.

Sweetcorn

Plants sown in April should be tall and sturdy with swelling cobs in leaf joints. The number of cobs on each plant will vary. This can be due to factors within your control, such as the variety, how early seed was sown or feeding regimes, but it can also be a matter of luck and how much sunshine any summer brings. If a variety regularly gives two or more cobs, make a note and stick with it. Growing in a polytunnel is all about maximizing the crop that you can get from your own particular space.

Corn becomes ready in a glut. Eat it fresh every day for a couple of weeks, with no more than half an hour from garden to pan. Make sure you pick cobs at the right moment, when they are sweet and juicy. Strip away the husk and silks, evict any earwigs and cook the cobs in a pan of boiling water for four minutes – that's all it takes to serve up delectable corn on the cob (of course a slather of butter and a sprinkling of pepper can enhance the taste too).

Leave ripe cobs unpicked and they will become starchy and far less sweet. Sweetcorn is a real taste of the summer, so binge and enjoy – don't let any of those golden beauties go to waste.

Sweetcorn

How to check if a corn cob is ripe
- A ripe cob should be fat and firm.
- Check that the silks on the end of the cob have turned brown and started to shrivel.
- Peel back the end of the cob to expose a few kernels. Press with a thumbnail to burst a kernel. If the fluid is milky and thin, the cob is perfect to pick. If the fluid is clear, it's still too early. If the kernel is dry, the cob is past its best.
- It's better to err on the side of early picking than to leave the crop to turn to starch. If a cob looks OK, pick it, cook it and eat it. If it is slightly unripe it will still taste good, but leave other cobs to ripen for a few more days.

☑ Some cobs will not have a full complement of kernels. This will have been determined weeks ago when pollination took place. Never leave cobs on the plant in the hope that they might grow more kernels. It just doesn't work that way. A half-filled cob still tastes pretty good!

Poorly pollinated corn cobs

Pumpkins

Winter potatoes
If you planted a few seed potatoes at the end of July, they should produce plenty of green leaf this month. There is still time to plant a few potatoes in containers in early August, but crops will be smaller.

Keep earthing up around the stem as plants grow; use compost to top up containers. The more stem that is buried, the less chance there is of potatoes turning green.

Watch out for blight, which can be a real problem with non-resistant varieties.

Pumpkins and squash
These plants ramble and the foliage may threaten to swamp other plants. Be ruthless: cut off a few leaves, once fruits are set, and train

stems to run where they cause the least problems. Stems can loop around on themselves if necessary. Depending on the variety, there may be three or four pumpkins starting to swell on each plant. Lift fruit carefully and slip a board, tile or slate underneath. This prevents the flesh rotting where it touches against damp soil.

Pumpkins and squash under cover ripen much faster than ones grown outdoors, and they may be ready by the end of the month. Once the fruit has stopped swelling and has reached a good colour, and the skin is firm, harvest each one with an inch of stem attached. Remove the haulms to free up space for other crops. Pumpkins will keep for months in a cool, frost-free shed, but squash is best eaten within a few weeks.

Broccoli

Young plants will be large enough to put out in the border soil in August. Try interplanting with another crop, such as sweetcorn, if space is limited. The corn will provide some shade and you can still harvest cobs while the broccoli is growing. Just be careful not to break the brittle corn stems. Once the corn has finished producing, you can remove the stalks and leave the broccoli to grow on unrestricted.

Plant broccoli plants 45cm/18in apart with 60cm/24in between rows. Add a scattering of lime if the soil is acid, but plants will do well on the nutrients left by the previous crop.

☑ Try sowing calabrese for a fast autumn crop.

Peppers

Ripening peppers 'Gypsy'

Sweet peppers should be covered in fruit at several stages. Large green peppers will ripen, to red or orange, if left on the plant. A few varieties ripen to more unusual colours, but it can be part of the fun to see what shades come out of a mixed pepper patch. Picking fruit at the green stage is supposed to allow more flowers to set fruit. However, it makes most sense to pick peppers when the person eating them thinks they taste best – some people hate them green and love them red, others love the green ones. Either way, there should be plenty of fruit for a few months yet. Use string or twigs to provide extra support if necessary. An unsupported limb laden with peppers can snap from the main stem, wasting most of the fruit.

Peppers need a lot of potash, so scatter wood ash, or apply a seaweed-based feed while fruit is swelling on the plants. They also like plenty of sunshine, so don't grow plants in the shade of tall crops. If light is short, remember the aluminium foil trick mentioned in July. Poor air circulation, low temperatures and lack of sun are the main reasons for peppers failing on the plant.

Chilli peppers are slower to produce fruit than their sweeter relatives. They also need plenty of sun to build up a hot taste. In a sunny position they will produce fiery little monsters until hard frosts kick in. Remember that red chillies tend to be hotter than green ones and that the hotter the growing temperature the hotter the fruit. Always taste a tiny scrap first, to check if a variety is a real scorcher.

Aubergines

These can also benefit from an aluminium foil mulch. Just make sure the ground doesn't dry out too much underneath.

Fruit should be swelling nicely and the first aubergines might be ready for picking this month. Be sure to harvest while the skin is firm and shiny. You will need to watch out for sharp spines on the stem, as these can give a nasty prick. Cut through the stem with a knife or clippers. Don't just tug on the plant, as roots may be damaged.

August is 'make or break' month for this temperamental vegetable. Some people grow aubergines without any problem; other people just can't seem to get them to work. Poor fruit set can be due to low temperatures, poor feeding or poor pollination (or all three at once). If no fruit has set, dampen a paintbrush and transfer pollen as early in the month as possible.

If we get a hot, late summer, it's still possible to get late fruit. Feed with a seaweed-based liquid feed and apply well-rotted horse manure as a mulch around the aubergine plants. Keep the soil moist but not soggy. There are no guarantees, but this treatment might do the trick.

☑ Remember to spray water over the leaves every day in hot, dry conditions. This will reduce problems with red spider mite.

TOP: Aubergine fruit and flowers
BOTTOM: Grapes starting to ripen

Grape vines

A grape vine in late August is a wonderful sight. Dangling bunches of fruit stretch all along the vine. Black varieties start to darken in colour and all will sweeten up if they get maximum exposure to the sun.

Water around roots, trim any leaves that shade bunches, remove any mouldy grapes and by all means taste a few ripe-looking ones to see when the first bunches are ready to eat. Real sweetness may not kick in until September, but it's always worth sampling at an early stage.

French beans

Climbing French beans do particularly well under cover and can continue to crop for a few weeks yet, but if they are blocking too much light, the end of August might be time to remove them for the sake of other crops. It's a question of judgement and balancing what is gained with what is lost.

Don't forget the two rules of polytunnel growing in the summer months

- **Water** regularly and carefully according to the demands of each crop. Nothing grows well in dry soil. If the atmosphere is very dry, hose down paths and mist overhead for moisture-loving plants.

TOP: Climbing French beans
MIDDLE: Lots of tomatoes
BOTTOM: Basil

• **Ventilate** and allow air to circulate between plants. Doors may well be left open day and night, or at least they should be opened as soon as the sun shines. Overheating can kill plants! Cut back foliage to allow air to move freely. Damp, muggy, overheated conditions can lead to lots of problems with moulds and mildews.

☑ If August is wet and there is nowhere to dry your **onion** crop, bring the bulbs into the polytunnel. Spread them around in any available space, or hang bunches from the framework. Don't spray the bulbs with water and don't leave them more than a couple of weeks. The environment is usually too moist for ongoing storage, but some useful drying can be done while the weather is wet outside.

Enjoy the August harvest
French beans
Grapes
Sweetcorn
Tomatoes
Aubergines
Peppers
Basil
Melons
Cucumbers
Salad leaves
Spinach
Courgettes
Pumpkin and squash

Some harvesting hints
• Regular harvesting is essential in order to keep plants cropping. During holidays ask a neighbour to do the job rather than leave things unpicked.
• Pick everything as it ripens. Look under leaves for lurking monsters and don't let **salad** crops bolt.
• Remember to keep nipping the top leaves from **basil** plants, so that they don't get a chance to flower.
• Eat sweetcorn over a short period before sugar turns to starch.

SEPTEMBER

September sees a subtle change inside the polytunnel. Temperatures may still be high and the harvest will keep rolling in, but many summer plants start to look tatty and some show signs of disease. Plants aim to set seed where possible and the clock is ticking. This may result in small distorted cucumbers that seem to be more seed than flesh; in tomatoes falling prematurely from the plant and splitting open to drop seed on the soil; in basil trying to form more flowers than leaves. Many summer crops will continue for weeks if the weather is halfway decent, but be vigilant for signs of disease, clear failing plants and fill empty spaces with winter crops.

Weather report

Sometimes September can feel more like summer than August does, but don't be fooled! Autumn has arrived, although it's never possible to predict exactly when the season will bare its teeth. The days are shortening, night temperatures are dropping and the first frost might arrive before the month is out. Strong gales can batter the country around the time of the equinox, so if the polytunnel is to survive unscathed make sure all rips are fixed, all doors are closed and no branches are likely to fall.

NOTE: At this time of year, northern gardens can be as much as three weeks ahead of those in the south. Flip between September and October tasks to determine the best work plan.

September polytunnel

September jobs in brief

Reduce watering
Ventilate on hot days
Close doors at night
Keep sowing for winter and spring crops
Plant out earlier sowings as space clears
Remove all lower leaves of tomato plants
Remove old, diseased and unproductive plants
Prepare liquid feeds for the winter
Keep harvesting
Keep checking for pests and diseases

Time to sow

Mizuna	Oriental greens
Mibuna	Spring cabbage
Rocket	Florence fennel
Land cress	Spinach beet
Lamb's lettuce	Kale
Any favourite winter salad leaves	Kohl rabi
Winter lettuce	Early carrot varieties
Winter turnip	

Keep sowing and planting

There are still plenty of seeds that you can start in pots or put into the ground this month. Even if you made sowings in July or August, a further sowing in September will ensure plenty of pickings spread over the months to come. The perfect timing for sowing can change from year to year. In a hot autumn, plants grow faster and for longer, before cold weather halts growth, so earlier sowings may reach maturity much sooner than planned. Look on extra sowings as an insurance policy to make sure there is plenty to harvest over the next six months.

Keep sowing lettuce and salad leaves

- Sow a **winter turnip** variety, such as 'Noir d'Hiver' – a delicious creamy root. 'Snowball' turnips also seem to survive the cold. Sow directly into a 1cm/½in -deep drill. Sow thickly, but be prepared to thin seedlings out; otherwise plants will grow lots of leaf at the expense of roots.
- Make another sowing of **winter lettuce** varieties in pots early this month. This sowing is crucial for a good supply right into the spring. Later sowings often germinate poorly and growth can slow down within a few weeks. It's important to get enough lettuce seedlings off to a good start in September, so that they can become established before soil temperatures fall too low.
- Make sowings of salad leaves such as **mizuna, mibuna, rocket** and **lamb's lettuce (corn salad)** this month. Prepare the ground well by digging in compost to provide nutrients and hold moisture. Sow in 1cm/½in-deep drills, about 30cm/12in apart, and mark the rows with sticks and string. These sowings will provide pickings for many

months to come, even through until April or May next year. These crops are all extremely hardy and will survive prolonged periods of temperatures below 0°C/32°F. Leaves may flop a little, but they perk up once temperatures rise. Salad leaves also do very well in large pots and containers.

- For a peppery taste, sow a row of an **oriental leaf** mixture or a salad blend containing something like spinach, mustard and kale. Young leaves can be used in salads, but older ones taste best when cooked.
- Southern gardens can get a good spring crop of early **carrots** if you sow seed in the polytunnel now. These will take about three weeks to germinate, so should be up before soil temperatures drop too low. Slugs and snails are less active as temperatures fall, but seedlings will still need some protection when they emerge.
- It is perfectly possible to have a supply of fresh **fennel** bulbs to eat right through the winter and into the spring. These make a wonderful and somewhat exotic change from winter greens. Fennel sown in early August should be ready to harvest in mid-winter. Early September sowings will make slower growth, but will still produce a spring crop that stands well into April, or even May. Plants can survive short periods of temperatures below 0°C/32°F in an unheated polytunnel and will still go on to produce good fleshy bulbs. They may stop growing for a while, and they may fail altogether if plants freeze solid in an exceptionally cold year, but in an average winter they will do fine. Sow fennel seed, such as 'Finale', 'Tauro' or 'Victoria', in pots of good compost. Germination should take only a few days at 15–20°C/59–68°F. Don't let seedlings dry out. Plant out into a damp rich soil when they are 10cm/4in tall. Fennel doesn't suffer ill effects from transplanting provided roots are kept as intact as possible and plants are not allowed to become potbound.
- **Pak choi** sown in trays last month can be planted out now, as can **spinach** and **spinach beet**. There is still time to make another sowing of these in early September.
- July or August sowings of **lettuce, kohl rabi, spring cabbage, beetroot,** etc., will be ready for planting out as soon as there is space. Clear any crops that have finished producing and be ruthless: it is better to replant, and have a full crop of winter lettuce in December, than to cherish a block of sweetcorn that has done its work and may never manage to ripen the last part-formed cobs. Winter crops need to get as much growing done as possible over the next few weeks, while the soil is still warm. Late sowings may not make a full-sized plant before the winter chills set in, but don't worry: they will usually start growing again in the New Year to give a spring crop.
- **Swiss chard** sown last month can also be planted out as crops clear. Chard grows quite large, so allow 30cm/12in between plants.
- It's worth planting a couple of **broccoli** and **kale** plants in the polytunnel in early September. These will grow quickly with the extra protection, and will crop ahead of those grown outdoors. Plants can be kept outside in a holding bed until space clears in the polytunnel. Just be careful not to damage roots when transplanting. Plant them 60cm/24in apart in the border soil. Don't add any extra feed – they will do well enough on what is left behind from the previous crop. Scatter lime or wood ash on the surface if soil is acid.

Broccoli and winter lettuce

☑ Watch out for cutworm eating through the base of newly planted lettuce and brassicas. If a plant suddenly keels over and dies, poke around in the soil near by until you find a greyish caterpillar about 4cm/1½in long. This will be the culprit, but fortunately you only usually find one at a time. Dispose of it and plant out a new seedling to fill the gap.

Air and water

September can be a tricky month. In some ways it mimics the spring with the potential for cold nights and warm days. Correct **ventilation** is vital for crop health, so it's back to opening doors during the day and closing them again before night falls. If there's no wind and it's not baking hot, open just one door. If a gale blows up, keep both doors shut. If it is windy but sunny, and polytunnel temperatures soar, open both doors to let air move through without harming the structure. Make sure catches are sound and open doors are securely propped, so that winds can't batter them off their hinges.

Reduce **watering** in September, even if the month is warm. Don't leave any plant thirsty, and particularly if fruit is swelling, but don't flood the soil.

Strawberries

If you pegged runners down into 8cm/3in pots in July, the young plants will need to be potted into 20cm/8in pots in September. Use compost from the garden heap to fill the pots. Don't add manure, as this contains high levels of nitrogen, and if there is too much nitrogen, plants will grow leaf at the expense of fruit. Spread roots evenly around the pot and don't bury the stem. Remove any discoloured leaves, but take care not to damage the growing point. The pots will stay outside the polytunnel, where they can be touched by frost before being moved back inside in a few months' time.

Tomatoes

Tomato plants should be covered with fruit in all shapes and sizes. Some plants will keep cropping for a month or two more, but maybe not all of them. In general, large-fruiting tomato varieties take the longest to ripen, and may well be at their best this month, but cherry varieties are the most likely to keep cropping through to December.

Lots of tomatoes

• Pick up fallen fruit before it spills seed, and try to keep new growth under control. Plants may outgrow the individual support provided, but they will be flexible enough to bend round to tie into a neighbouring pole.

• Stop feeding plants in September and reduce watering to a minimum. Too much water will make fruit thin skinned and more likely to split.

• Remove any diseased leaves and ones from the lower two-thirds of the stem. Plants will look stripped of leaves, but fruit should get as much sunlight as possible.

• If any plant looks badly diseased (see Part 5) or has collapsed, remove it altogether, trying not to spread any spores. Watch out for signs of blight. Spores can blow in through open doors. First indicators are large dark spots that can merge to blacken the whole leaf (smaller, regular spots may be caused by virus disease, which is much less of a problem). Fruit develops brown patches that soon rot. Once fruit is infected there isn't a cure, but the spread of the disease can be slowed down. Remove any affected leaves and fruit as soon as you see symptoms. Swift action is the key – remove anything that might produce spores to infect other plants.

☑ At this time of year, I leave side shoots to grow on near the top of tomato plants and only cut out the growing point if there are signs of disease. Leaving a few side shoots now means there is a greater chance that plants will crop right through the autumn.

Peppers

These plants come into their own over the next few weeks, with sweet peppers ripening to a glorious array of yellows, oranges, purples and reds. Plants will need support to avoid damage to laden stems. Use sticks and plenty of thick string, so that branches don't snap across the ties.

Peppers come into their own

If sunshine levels are low, spread aluminium foil underneath the plants to reflect more light (see July). Chilli varieties need lots of sun for fruit to ripen and build up heat. If plants are in pots, it is still possible to wrap some foil underneath.

Pepper plants will continue to flower for the next few months. If the weather is mild, these flowers will produce useful fruits. Keep tapping branches gently to ensure pollination and keep the soil damp, so that fruit can swell. Plants should continue to crop for a few months yet.

Check fruit regularly and watch out for slugs. A small hole on the outside of a pepper can mean that the inside is ruined by a single resident pest. Pick fruit when green if preferred, or leave them to ripen on the plant for a sweeter flavour.

☑ Pot-grown chilli varieties can be brought into the house at the end of September. Provided they haven't been touched by frost, these plants will grow well in a sunny window. They look beautiful and fruit will ripen right through the winter. In fact, I've even dug up plants from the polytunnel soil to bring indoors. Make sure you get as intact a root ball as possible and use a large pot.

Melons

In a hot September it is still possible for some fruits to ripen. These should be supported in nets and picked when ripe. However, if plants only start to flower this month then it's almost certainly too late to get a crop. If leaves start to brown and the stems rot, evict the lot.

Grape vines

Black grapes will show their true colour early in September and delicious bunches should be dangling from the vine. Grapes need sun to ripen fully, and plenty of air

TOP: Ripe grapes
BOTTOM: Grey
mould on grapes

to avoid disease, so cut back surplus leaves. Sample a grape or two to see if a bunch is ripe before harvesting. The grape should be plump and juicy; the skin should be well coloured with a bloom that fades when wet and reappears when dry. If one grape passes the test, pick the whole bunch and enjoy!

In a cold damp summer it can be hard to avoid moulds and mildews in the humid environment of a polytunnel. Remove any bunches of grapes that show signs of attack. This at least reduces the number of spores in the air and, if the weather improves, the rest of the crop may escape unscathed. If the whole crop starts to moulder, pick and dispose of all the bunches. This may be disheartening, but it isn't as bad as the constant sight and smell of mouldy grapes.

☑ Don't dispose of grapes on an open compost heap. Dogs love to eat them, but they can cause renal failure.

☑ Tightly packed bunches of grapes can hide woodlice and earwigs in their heart. If you want to avoid creepy crawlies galloping around the fruit platter, submerge such bunches in a bowl of water before serving.

Cucumbers

Give plants a health check and remove any discoloured leaves. If plants are still growing, earth up around the base of the stem with fresh compost. Water regularly and apply a liquid feed if plants are cropping well and need a nutrient boost. Keep picking cucumbers even if they are small and curled into unusual shapes. They will still taste good and regular picking keeps plants producing as long as the weather is kind.

Early sowings can crop right through September if the month is warm, but they will look less healthy than later-sown plants. The latter can crop well into October, but all plants will begin to fail at the first hint of cold weather; an unseasonable early frost, or even just a cold night, can finish them off. Remove failing plants immediately and use the space for other crops.

☑ If you have grown cucumbers in a hotbed, you can fill this with beetroot plants when you have removed the cucumbers. Or spread the contents as a mulch for other crops.

Aubergines

An aubergine plant full of plump, purple fruit is possibly a more glorious sight than one full of flowers! The size of individual fruits may vary, so watch out for other signs to check for ripeness: fruit will have stopped growing; the skin will be taut and will have a good colour and a healthy bloom; if squeezed gently, there will be a bit of 'give' to the flesh, but it should still be firm.

If no fruit has set and flowers turn brown, it's time to call it a day and uproot the lot. Even if fruit sets in September, it is unlikely to reach any decent size at this late stage. If you didn't pollinate flowers with a soft paintbrush in early summer, make a note to do so next year.

Check ailing plants for webs on the leaves, as red spider mite can be the reason for plant failure.

☑ Cut aubergines from the plant with a short length of stem attached, but watch out for sharp spines.

Overwintered onions

It may seem strange to advocate growing such a hardy plant in a polytunnel, but if space is available, it's worth considering. Overwintered onion sets such as 'Radar' or 'Senshu Yellow' can be planted from mid-September to mid-October. When grown outdoors, they are subject to all the weather that a cold winter can throw at them. In a polytunnel, they can maintain a steadier rate of growth right through the winter. Sets planted now will make reasonable-sized onions in March or April. These shouldn't be considered a replacement for outdoor crops, since they should be lifted when small in order to free up space, but they are sweet and delicious at a time of year when stored onions might be coming to an end.

Basil

A basil patch can look a bit of a mess in September and it's hard to keep one picking ahead of the flowering spikes. Sweet basil isn't tolerant of cold. Plants will start to drop leaves and turn brown as soon as the first frost arrives. Plants towards the middle of the tunnel may last longer than those next to the polythene and they don't all have to be removed at the same time. Remove failing plants and strip them of any remaining green leaves.

☑ You may well have a basil plant, or two, growing in pots in the kitchen. If not, you can always dig up a healthy plant, with an intact root ball, at the beginning of September, put it in a large pot and bring it to a sunny kitchen window to grow on through the winter. Or sow a few seeds in a pot indoors.

Butternut squash

Butternut squash seems to take a week or two longer for fruit to ripen than other pumpkins and squash. However, at some point in September, fruits should have swollen to give decent-sized squash. When the fruit stops swelling, it needs plenty of sunshine to ripen and for the skin to firm up. Cut back all leaves that overshadow the fruit. Once the skin is firm and has a blush of colour, harvest with a length of stem attached.

Butternut squash

☑ Leave harvested fruit in the polytunnel for a week or so to develop more flavour before using, but don't try to store for too long. I don't know why, but I find that pumpkins and squash grown in a polytunnel don't keep quite as long as those grown outdoors.

Making comfrey
liquid feed

September harvest

Liquid feed

Plants in a polytunnel keep growing for more of the winter than ones grown outdoors. Any bit of sunshine can raise soil temperature and boost growth. Make a brew of liquid feed in the autumn and it will be perfect to give plants a kick-start in the early months of next year. If comfrey or nettles are growing in the garden, cut them now and put them to soak in a bin full of water. If possible, add some seaweed too. All are rich in minerals and will produce an excellent liquid feed (see Part 7).

Enjoy the September harvest

Tomatoes	Lettuce
Aubergines	Salad leaves
Cucumbers	French beans
Peppers	Melons
Grapes	Butternut squash
Basil	Courgettes
Sweetcorn	

Some harvesting hints

- The **grape** harvest should be in full swing. Check for ripeness before picking a bunch and don't let fruit go past its best.
- Pick **basil** regularly and try to stop plants from flowering. There won't be many more pickings left.
- Keep up with the harvesting and never despair at yet another basketful of **tomatoes**. It's better to pick regularly, and keep plants cropping, than to leave overripe fruit to drop to the ground. Even in an Indian summer, the hot weeks are numbered. If frosts arrive before the end of the month, growth will be slowed and the glut will start to tail off. The aim is to keep plants in the best possible condition, in the hope that they will continue to crop for a few weeks yet. So pick, eat, freeze, preserve and give away, but don't waste those beautiful baskets of fruit and veg.
- If you didn't evict the **courgette** plant in summer, don't do so now. It will keep producing tasty small fruit long after the outdoor ones have died back.
- Pick chillies when green for a milder flavour. Leave them to ripen to red if you like them hot!

OCTOBER

Work in the polytunnel starts to wind down in October. There are still plenty of things to do, but little has the same urgency as in the spring and summer months. Keep harvesting, keep an eye out for problems, clear exhausted plants and remember to get young plants into the ground. There are some jobs that can be spread over the next three or four months, but in order to get ahead of the game it's a good idea to start the process of the big tidy-up.

Weather report

The first half of October might be warm and settled, but the second half of the month often arrives with the full force of winter at its back. The weather can turn cold and very wet. There will almost certainly be frosts this month and if there were storms at the end of September, these may well persist. In northern parts of the UK the weather can be as much as one month closer to winter than the south.

October jobs in brief

Tidy up
Repair polythene, frames and doors
Get most of the winter and early spring crops sown or planted
Remove dead and diseased foliage, or whole plants that have finished cropping
Provide extra coverings to extend the growing season
Watch out for pests and diseases
Keep doors closed in strong winds
Reduce ventilation and watering, according to daytime temperatures
Plant bulbs in pots
Keep harvesting

October polytunnel

Time to sow

Mibuna	Oriental green mixes
Mizuna	Kohl rabi
Rocket	Early carrots
Land cress	Garlic
Winter lettuce varieties	Overwintered onion sets
Spinach	Mangetout peas

October sowing

- Sow **salad leaves** early in the month. Most of these will do extremely well from an October sowing and should crop from January on.
- **Lettuce, kohl rabi** and **carrots** sown now may not make much growth if cold weather sets in. In fact, in a really cold winter, they might sit at the seedling stage for several weeks. However, it's still worth trying an October sowing. In some winters these plants will go on to produce excellent crops. Use an early variety of **carrot** such as 'Amsterdam Forcing' or 'Early Nantes'. Sow seed thickly in drills in the border or, if you haven't much room, sow in a large flowerpot. Seed needs a little warmth to germinate, but that should be possible with a bit of October sun. Once seedlings are up they are fairly hardy, although an extra layer of fleece can be of use. Carrot seedlings always need protection from slugs. These beasts can stay active in the polytunnel in mild winter months.

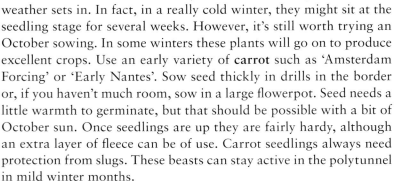

Carrot seedlings

- Sow **mangetout peas** in pots of good compost (sowing *in situ* is another option, but pots seem to work best) at the end of the month. Cover the pots with a layer of bubble wrap or fleece, and keep them out of the way of rodents if these are a problem. Seed doesn't need any extra warmth to germinate and the first green leaves should appear in a couple of weeks. If the weather is cold be patient, as germination might take a little longer. These plants will go on to produce a first early taste of summer. Pods should be ready to harvest from April on.

Planting garlic

☑ I use the mangetout pea variety 'Oregon Sugar Pod' and find this successfully survives temperatures below 0°C/32°F when grown in a polytunnel. Other varieties may be as good, but I can't vouch for them and seed packets don't mention autumn sowing. If you have a favourite, give it a try.

- Autumn-planting varieties of **garlic** are often put outdoors this month, but it's worth growing a few plants in the polytunnel. These come up much faster than the outdoor ones and in a mild year you may get small useful bulbs in March. If there is space to leave them to grow on, the result can be large bulbs, with bigger cloves than those grown outdoors. Push individual cloves into the soil, allowing 15cm/6in between each one.

☑ Garlic grows well in large pots in the polytunnel. You can stand these outdoors to grow on as the weather warms up, or you can plant out the young plants in the garden to fill gaps in rows.

The big tidy-up

Over the next three or four months, the polytunnel should be put in order so that everything is ready for the coming year. This is usually a matter of clearing all debris, scrubbing benches and frames, as well as cleaning the polythene. It might also mean washing used pots, repairing damage to the structure and sweeping pathways. The aim is to get everything as clean, clear and sound as possible. This enables the plants that are still growing to have the best chance of producing healthy crops. It also means that problems are less likely to be carried through from one year to the next.

Not all tidying has to be done in October, but it is a good idea to make a start. A diligent gardener might wash all pots this month; a busy one might stack them in the shed to wash in the New Year. That doesn't matter much as long as the pots get washed. What does matter is the overall structural integrity of the polytunnel. Check over everything and repair holes before they spread and split the polythene in two (see January).

If doors need repairing, or replacing, do the job before they fail altogether in a winter storm.

Tomatoes

Plants should still have plenty of ripening fruit at the beginning of the month, but things can change dramatically over thirty-one days. If freezing nights are the norm, tomato plants will edge towards their end, but if an Indian summer persists, plants will continue to crop for several weeks yet. A few cool nights can be a positive thing: moulds and mildews love warm damp conditions and, although they won't disappear altogether, lower temperatures can stop them in their tracks. Remove any diseased or discoloured leaves and expose remaining fruit to as much light as possible. Water plants very sparingly at this end of the year, and only when the surface of the soil has dried out.

Tomatoes may not ripen at this end of the year

Green trusses start to have a distinctly different colour as temperatures drop: they are paler, and may never ripen on the plant.

Don't be in a rush to pull up plants, unless they are badly diseased. If cherry varieties survive a short cold snap, they often pick up and continue to ripen fruit. In milder areas it is perfectly possible to eat fresh cherry tomatoes in December.

Aubergines

These can still fruit into October in warm areas and if the weather is kind. Once you have picked all the fruit, remove the plants. If red spider mite was a problem it may be wise to burn affected plants.

☑ To keep tender plants growing – and often temperatures might rise again after a temporary dip – provide an extra layer of covering, such as fleece or a cloche, when a cold night is forecast. In a really cold month there may be no other option than to accept the end of some summer crops, but it is worth trying to keep things going for as long as possible.

Cucumbers

Cucumbers may have hung on until October, but they won't last beyond this month. Leaves will turn brown and plants flop at the first hard frost. Pick any remaining fruit, remove whole plants and scrub out any containers that you will use again next year.

NOTE: Outdoor varieties that are grown in the polytunnel will often crop for longer than all-female ones bred for the glasshouse.

Potatoes

Second-cropping potatoes planted in July should be growing well and will begin to flower by the end of the month. Leaves should be a healthy green colour with no signs of blight. (If tomatoes show signs of this disease, it won't be long before any non-resistant varieties of potato are also affected.) Try covering potato plants with an extra layer or two of fleece, or use clear polythene. Even though they are already under cover, this will keep plants warm and prevent blight spores from landing on the leaves. Don't forget to water potatoes grown in containers. Although other areas of the polytunnel may require less water, potatoes will still need enough to swell a good crop. Try not to splash the foliage when watering.

Peppers

Both sweet and chilli peppers come into their own at this end of the year. There should be delicious tasty fruit all through this month and on into the next. Most fruit ripens to a lovely deep red and chilli peppers begin to really get hot with any bit of sunshine – remember red chilli peppers are always hotter than the green version.

Peppers galore

It's extraordinary that pepper plants, which needed plenty of heat to start them off when young, can withstand such temperature dips in the autumn. Leaves may start to fall from the plants and there is little that can be done about this, but peppers will continue to ripen even though foliage is sparse. Water sparingly at this end of the year and watch out for slug damage and rotting fruit.

☑ Pick peppers as and when you need them. They tend to soften and wrinkle if a lot are picked and stored.

Courgettes

Plants will look really tatty after cropping for so many months, but don't dig them up too soon.

It's worth waiting for the one or two small courgettes a week, provided the space isn't needed for other crops. The first really cold night might see an end to production: lift plants at that point and put them on the compost heap.

French beans

A July sowing of dwarf beans should crop well into October. Climbing French varieties might still be cropping from a spring sowing, but the pods get tough after so many months. When the harvest isn't worth the space that the crop is taking, cut off stems at ground level, and remove the haulms and any fallen leaves.

Drying French beans

☑ Extract the beans out of any tough pods. You can use these fresh, or dry them for use over the next few months.

Grapes

Bunches will continue to ripen in a warm, sunny October, but harvest grapes while the fruit is still sound. The polytunnel can begin to smell like a winery if grapes start to split, and insects will feast on overripe fruit. Remove bunches that are past their best and pick up all fallen grapes.

Leaves will turn a glorious colour in October. Pick up ones that fall, but enjoy the display of those on the vine for a week or two yet.

Florence fennel

If you sowed fennel in pots in the previous months, get it into the ground before the end of October, with plants 20cm/8in apart and 30cm/12in between rows. If the soil is poor, dig compost into the plot before planting. Don't let plants go short of water; otherwise they may run to seed. This plant is surprisingly hardy and will grow on for weeks yet. Watch out for slugs, which can stay active for longer in the warmer conditions of a polytunnel. These are only a problem when plants are small.

Fennel will crop over a long period. From an August sowing, bulbs can be harvested from December to May. The foliage can be used at any time, provided a plant is never stripped of leaves. Plants might need extra coverings if temperatures fall below 0°C/32°F.

Wood ash helps raise soil pH

Spring cabbage

Late sowings of spring cabbage should be planted out in October. Plants should be 45cm/18in apart – they might seem small and a bit spindly, but they will come into their own and fill out to justify the spacing in the spring. Choose a cool day and transplant in the evening, making sure the young plants are thoroughly watered in. If the soil is acid, add lime or wood ash to raise pH.

Cabbages love the spent manure from a cucumber hotbed spread around as a mulch (although lime and manure shouldn't be allowed to mix). The nitrogen from the manure can lead to soft, leafy growth, but this is seldom a problem for cabbages in a polytunnel.

Plenty of autumn
and winter crops

Brassicas transplant well and don't mind root disturbance. If buying in young cabbage plants, avoid limp specimens and always check for signs of clubroot disease – lumps and bumps that distort the roots. Spring cabbage can be grown outdoors, but plants produce earlier, lush, soft leaves if they are grown in the polytunnel.

Winter crops

All young plants should be growing well from summer sowings. Keep them weeded and watered. They should be well coloured and healthy. Look out for slug damage. In a mild autumn these pests can destroy small seedlings, but they might also slide into the folds of a cabbage to survive the winter. Removing and destroying them now can avoid a lot of damage in the months ahead.

Lettuce and **Swiss chard**, sown in trays in August, should go into their final homes as crops clear from the polytunnel. Both will manage on the leftovers from a previously manured crop, but they like the soil to be dug over and loose. Allow plenty of room around chard plants, as they can be prone to moulds if overcrowded.

NOTE: Growing winter lettuce in too rich a soil can lead to problems with mildew.

Parsley does well in the polytunnel throughout the winter months. Plants raised from seed can be planted in the border or in large pots.

☑ Pots of parsley plants can often be found in the fruit and vegetable section of the supermarket. If the plants are short and sturdy they will thrive when planted out in the polytunnel. Avoid overcrowded pots with tall leggy plants.

Why not plant a few bulbs?

Plant spring-flowering bulbs in pots in the polytunnel for the earliest blooms. You can't eat them, but they look so lovely that they are worth a mention. Containers can be moved outdoors in the spring, but in the meantime, the foliage will benefit from the protection of the polytunnel.

Air and water

Ventilation now is as important as ever. Hot humid conditions encourage disease, but a cold wind blowing through can knock plants back. Open doors on hot days and keep them closed when temperatures fall. Remember that a door can be propped ajar to allow some ventilation, while reducing wind damage on cooler days. Always close doors overnight in October.

Watering should be reduced to a minimum now, but don't let plants in containers dry out.

Enjoy the October harvest

Basil
Cucumbers
Peppers
Aubergines
Tomatoes
French beans
Grapes
Fennel
Salad leaves
Lettuce
Spinach
Courgettes
Pak choi

October harvest

Some harvesting hints

- Some of the July sowings may have grown into large plants. Start picking the large outer leaves of **Swiss chard, spinach, kale**, etc., if desired. In any case these will often discolour and drop from the plants as the winter rolls on.
- Enjoy **pak choi** while the stems are young and juicy. This isn't a very hardy plant and it may fail as the weather chills.
- When you lift tender plants, strip off all viable fruits, pods, etc. Green **tomatoes** will ripen indoors if left with a banana or ripe tomato to speed up the process.

Ruby chard

NOVEMBER

It can be tempting to ignore the polytunnel for the next couple of months, especially if the weather is miserable. If a complete clear-up, plant-out, scrub-down and eviction of old plants took place in October, it might be possible to do little work other than harvesting in November, but few gardeners are that organized. Even in the coldest months, there are plenty of things that can be done to get the best out of a polytunnel. Get out there! Keep tidying! Try sowing broad beans, planting out peas or using water barrels for warmth. A polytunnel offers protection from the elements and on bright days it can be quite warm. Put in a few hours per week in November and maybe December will be an easier month.

Weather report

If the winter months are in any way true to form, November should bring an abundance of rain and a few gales or, at the very least, some strong winds. Bitterly cold weather, hard frosts and the first snow falls are also possibilities. Soil in the poytunnel will be slower to cool down than that outdoors, but once it drops below 5°C/41°F plant growth will stop.

November
polytunnel

November jobs in brief

Bring water barrels into the polytunnel

Sow broad beans and peas

Plant out September and October sowings started in pots

Remove all dead and diseased foliage

Clear summer crops that have stopped producing

Check for storm damage

Start feeding the soil

Water very sparingly

Stake tall plants

Plant a grape vine

Time to sow

Broad beans	Mibuna
Mangetout peas	Rocket
Winter lettuce	Mustard greens
Mizuna	Early carrots

Keep planting out

Late sowings

Anything that is sown in November will grow very slowly and may not give a crop until well into the spring. However, these sowings will still give crops much earlier than similar sowings outdoors.

• Try sowing **broad beans** and **mangetout peas** in early November (if you have not done so in late October) and be the envy of other gardeners next spring. These plants should start to crop in April – about a month sooner than those sown outdoors. You can also sow winter-hardy, podding peas, but somehow these don't seem to crop any earlier than ones sown under a cloche outside.

Choose a hardy variety of bean, such as 'Aquadulce Claudia' or 'Super Aquadulce', and sow individual seeds in 8cm/3in pots. A cold-tolerant mangetout pea such as 'Oregon Sugar Pod' can be sown at four seeds per 10cm/4in pot, or more if you are using larger tubs. Lay seeds on the surface and push them down with a finger to the first knuckle joint, before covering with compost. Sow more seed than you need in case some fails. Cover with a layer of bubble polythene to give the best chance of germination. Don't provide any extra heat, as this can lead to weak plants that will not survive well in a hard winter.

Direct sowing in the soil is also an option, but always put a few extra seeds in pots, or at the ends of the row; these can be transplanted to fill gaps. Watch out for hungry mice and rats, who will dig up seed and eat it.

☑ I find that putting pea and bean pots in a large, clear plastic storage box (inside the polytunnel) works really well. It keeps slugs and mice at bay as well as providing a small bit of extra warmth.

• Rows of **rocket, mizuna, mibuna** and **mustard greens** seem able to survive temperatures as low as –7°C/19°F and still bounce back to produce prolific crops. Sowings in November will grow slowly, but should be ready for picking in late

Try sowing carrots
in a large pot

winter or early spring. Sow all these crops directly into the soil, as they do not transplant well.

• **Winter lettuce** can still be sown, but it's worth starting the seed off indoors. Put pots on a window ledge in a cool room, so that seedlings don't grow too 'soft'. Harden off before planting out in the polytunnel when seedlings are 3–4cm/1¼–1½in tall.

> ☑ In a mild winter you might have success with November sowings of early **carrots** and **kohl rabi**. Nothing is guaranteed, but it is always worth a try if you haven't made earlier sowings and you want a few extra crops.

Water barrels for warmth

If there was no frost in October, there will certainly be some in November. Plants should be frost free in the polytunnel, but many won't like the low temperatures. To raise temperatures slightly, it's worth filling a couple of barrels (or dustbins) with water inside the polytunnel. These will warm up with the heat of the sun during the day and slowly release heat through the night. The overall effect may be small, but any gain at this point of the year is worthwhile.

NOTE: A barrel will also be a handy source into which you can dip a watering can. Hosepipes may be frozen, or the outdoor water supply too chilly for sheltered plants.

Planting out

• Late sowings of **spring cabbage** can be planted out in early November. These will be ready to eat in late April or May. It might not be worth doing such a late planting in a small polytunnel, as you will need the space for summer crops before the cabbage has formed good heads.
• **Winter lettuce** is still worth planting, even in a small space. This will give good pickings next March or April, especially if you use the leaves while the plants are still small.
• **Spinach** and **kohl rabi** sown in trays last month should be planted out as soon as possible. Young roots need a little time to establish themselves in the soil before really low temperatures kick in.
• **Oriental greens**, sown last month, can grow thick and fast. If plants need more space, thin and transplant a few seedlings.
• **Mustard greens** and **kales** certainly suffer little harm from transplanting, so it's worth a try. Remember that this crop is primarily intended for picking while the leaves are small and sweet.

Tomatoes

Thin-skinned varieties may split as they ripen. Such fruit is still perfectly edible if used the same day. Moulds will grow in the exposed flesh if split fruit is allowed to fall or sit on the plant for several days. Small plum varieties seem to have slightly thicker skins, which don't split so easily, so they may give sound fruit for the longest time.

In a mild autumn, plants can grow on into December. They won't produce a lot of ripe fruit and the taste won't be quite the same as a summer sun-ripened tomato, but there is something satisfying about picking tomatoes from the polytunnel this late in the year. The downside of this is that any diseased foliage and fruit hang around for longer than is really sensible. To give the soil a chance to recover, it's best to pick all fruit (red, green or in-between) as soon as growth and ripening stop. Remove plants and be sure to scour the soil for any dropped fruit and leaves, as these can carry disease through into the next year's crop.

☑ If you have used canes or poles to support plants, remove these with care. A sudden upward jolt, as you pull them out of the ground, can damage the polythene.

Remember that you don't have to clear all plants on the same day. Leave the ones that are still cropping and remove the ones that have finished. Burn haulms if they are diseased, along with any fallen leaves; otherwise add them to the compost heap.

Bowls full of green tomatoes will ripen on a window ledge if you put one or two red ones in the bowl to speed up the process.

☑ Don't compost any fallen or spoiled tomato fruits. This can lead to a host of seedlings carrying disease into next year.

Peppers

Peppers will be enjoying their swan song this month, as they try to ripen through the shortening days. It's worth allowing peppers to ripen on the plant, even if the leaves look tatty and some start to drop. Fruit stays firmer this way and may even ripen in December, if the weather isn't too cold. Pick as needed early in the month, but harvest the lot if temperatures fall below 0°C/32°F. If plants freeze inside the polytunnel, the leaves will blacken and fruit will spoil.

Harvest all chilli peppers once they stop ripening. They freeze really well and they also dry if left on a plate in a warm room. Try freezing half and dry the rest – both forms are equally useful. Dried chillis keep for months if put in a screw-top jar.

Once picked, sweet peppers can finish ripening on a sunny window ledge, but use them quickly before they become too soft.

Ripe chilli peppers can be frozen or dried

Potatoes

Second-cropping varieties, planted in the summer, should be covered with a few layers of fleece. Even so, they will not survive too many frosts. The leaves and stems will turn brown, but the tubers should be safe and sound in the compost beneath. If you are saving these for Christmas, leave them undisturbed and they will lift from the compost as fresh tasting as any early spud.

Lettuce and salad leaves

Summer lettuce varieties may still be growing well, but it's worth picking these before they reach full size. If you leave them to grow bigger, they will start to rot as temperatures drop.

In a mild autumn, cut-and-come-again crops such as mizuna and mibuna can grow very fast. Pick leaves regularly; otherwise the plants will flower and the crop will finish much earlier than it should.

☑ If you are faced with a row of large floppy salad leaves, use scissors to cut them back. This will encourage new growth and will postpone flowering for a few more weeks.

Strawberries

These should be outdoors in pots, but don't ignore them altogether. Check to see that the plants are healthy. Cut off any discoloured leaves, nip out any errant flowers and top up compost if it has settled too low in the pots. They plants will come back into the polytunnel in a few weeks' time and you should look after them in the meantime.

Winter winds

Gales can be devastating at this end of the year. Check the structure of the polytunnel regularly, especially if there are any strong winds. Fallen branches or flying pieces of debris can puncture polythene. Pre-empt this by cutting overhanging branches and weighting down any materials that might take flight.

Remember that if wind blows straight into a structure, it must have a way to get out.

Feeding the soil

☑ Doors can blow open if latches are rattled for long enough. Put a heavy weight against the outside of the door to stop this happening.

Feed the soil

A healthy soil will grow healthy crops, but a lot is expected from the borders in a polytunnel. When one crop is lifted, another goes in, and constant demands are made on the soil. The borders don't contain an endless supply of nutrients. Although you can apply liquid and dried feeds, the soil will eventually run out of steam if it doesn't get a good bulky feed such as manure, compost or seaweed from time to time. November is a good time to do this: beds aren't so jam packed and there is plenty of time for the material to break down and be incorporated into the soil for the year ahead.

Spread the manure or compost around growing plants, or make a pile and spread it out as any patch clears. You can always dig it in at a later date. The important thing is to get a good bulk of lovely organic material into the soil.

NOTE: You can buy compost and manure in bags if you don't have access to a fresh supply.

Watering tips

The need for watering should be minimal in November. The water table rises in the land surrounding the polytunnel and borders should stay damp enough through the next few months. An occasional sprinkling of water will be required, but not much more. Containers will still need watering, as will any bed that is raised well above the outdoor soil level.

Water salad crops carefully. Too much water will make lettuce susceptible to grey mould, but too little water will make leaves bitter.

Staking tall plants

Tall plants, such as broccoli, kale or sprouts, need staking when they are grown in a polytunnel. They may not have to withstand the ravages of a winter gale, but plants can become top heavy. The whole plant can fall over and if roots are broken or pulled up, growth will be set back. Drive a stake into the ground and tie the stem to this at a minimum of two points – this prevents breakage across the tie.

Staking tall plants

Plant a grape vine

Vines can be rampant growers, so it's unwise to grow one in a tiny polytunnel, unless you grow it in a large pot and restrict growth to 1m/39in high. In a large tunnel, however, a vine trained upwards and along the ridge can do spectacularly well.

Ideally the vine should root outdoors and the stem is then trained inside. This can be done through a small hole in the polythene, with all edges of the hole securely taped. Alternatively, plant the vine just outside a door and train the stem around the door frame. This might leave a gap where the door closes against the stem. You can avoid this by cutting a notch in a wooden door or frame.

☑ Ouch! I can't bear to make any hole in the polythene, even though I have seen it successfully done. I always prefer to wind the vine around a door frame.

☑ Take a little time to select the variety of grape you plant. Ask what does well in your area and, if possible, sample some fruit from a mature vine. The vine will grow for many years. If you plant a small-fruited, seeded variety that is suitable for wine making when what you really wanted was a large, seedless, dessert one, you are sure to be disappointed.

Choose a sunny spot for planting the vine and preferably somewhere that doesn't dry out too quickly. Dig a hole about 45cm/18in square. Half fill this with compost before planting and top up with soil. The growing medium should be heading towards a pH of 7, so if the soil is too acid scatter a little lime over the surface. Plant the vine at the same level that it grew in the pot it was purchased in and water well if the soil is dry. Prune to leave three or four strong buds.

A grape vine requires some work to produce good crops, but there is nothing that can't be learned.

Holly time

Holly bushes are full of glorious red berries in November, but it won't be long before the blackbirds and fieldfares turn up for a late autumn feast. If you want to keep any berries for Christmas, now is the time to act. Cut a few laden branches, with plenty of woody stem at the lower end. Push the cut stem down into damp soil in the

Holly time!

November harvest

polytunnel. There should be enough moisture to keep the berries fresh until Christmas time.

Enjoy the November harvest

Sweet and chilli peppers	Spinach
Salad leaves	Kohl rabi
Lettuce	Pak choi
Oriental greens	Fennel
Tomatoes	Beetroot

Some harvesting hints

- In a mild year, some summer crops will struggle into November. It's unlikely there will be more than a few small **courgettes**, or the odd leaf of **basil**, but it can be worth leaving them to grow until they are killed by frost.
- The main pickings will be from **winter greens**, although late **peppers** and **tomatoes** can also put in a good show. Pick winter crops regularly but carefully. Growth will slow down through the winter and pick up again in the spring, by which time they will tolerate much harder picking.
- **Lettuce** plants from the same sowing grow at different rates at this end of the year. This is quite handy for spreading out the cropping season. Cut the biggest plants first, and always before they become bitter.

DECEMBER

Short days and cold weather can mean that little gets done in the polytunnel in December, but there's no harm in taking things easy for a few weeks. There are jobs that can be done, of course, but every gardener needs a break. If you leave most of the work for this month until January, little will suffer, but do take a regular walk around to harvest crops and to check that nothing needs immediate care. It's a great time to do a bit of armchair gardening too – reflect on the past year in the polytunnel, browse through some seed catalogues and start to draw up plans for the year ahead. Of course, if the sun shines and the polytunnel beckons, get out there and enjoy some winter gardening.

Weather report

December can be cold, wet and windy. Daytime temperatures might struggle to get above freezing and the days are so short that there hardly seems time to do anything in the polytunnel. Block draughts under doors and keep growing crops as warm as possible. The shortest day will pass by at the end of the month and new enthusiasm will build as the days start drawing out.

Still jobs to do in the December polytunnel

December jobs in brief

Plant out peas and beans
Plant a few early potatoes
Clear the last of the summer crops
Clean up and prune grape vines
Check the structure and make repairs
Order seeds
Think about fittings and fixtures
Wash pots
Look after the soil
Keep harvesting

Time to sow

Broad beans
Mangetout peas
Winter lettuce
Mizuna, mibuna, rocket

December sowing

This isn't the best month for sowing crops: days are short, light levels are low and soil temperatures can often be below the level that is required for growth. Having said that, it's always worth sowing a few salad leaves if spring crops are in short supply.

- Try sowing **mizuna, mibuna** and **rocket** in large pots rather than in the ground. Bring the pots into the house until the seeds germinate. After germination, move the pots back out to the polytunnel, with an extra layer of fleece on top. There should be plenty of pickings in a few weeks' time.
- It's still worth trying a sowing of mangetout peas this month. Sow plenty of seed, as some will not germinate. There should be plenty of plants to go out in late January or February.

How cold is cold?

Temperatures usually drop significantly in December and for the next couple of months growth will slow right down, or stop altogether. Plants can't grow at temperatures below 5°C/41°F and if they freeze solid, some of the less hardy ones won't survive. Polytunnel crops have the benefit of raised daytime temperatures on bright days. This will keep soil temperatures higher than those outdoors, but nights can drop below 0°C/32°F. It's worth investing in a maximum and minimum thermometer, which will give some idea of the temperature swings that plants in the polytunnel have to cope with. You can buffer them from the worst effects a little by using fleece, or cloches, as an extra layer of protection.

> ☑ I only use fleece in this way during really cold spells. Most plants should be pretty hardy at this end of the year and it is best to remove extra coverings if temperatures are above 0°C/32°F. This allows more light and air to reach plants, which means fewer problems with moulds and mildews.

Peas and beans

Mangetout peas and broad beans, sown in pots, will be ready for planting out when 5–8cm/2–3in tall. Dig a trench to a spade's depth and half fill this with compost from the garden heap. Fill the rest of the trench with soil. Place plants at the same depth at which they grew in the pot and don't bury any stem as this may lead to rot. Set a double row of peas 15cm/6in apart with approximately 5cm/2in between plants. If seeds were multiple-sown in pots, it is possible to loosen the compost and shuffle the plants apart to the correct spacing. Having said that, this isn't a precise science and mangetout peas do very well at closer spacings if that's how they work out.

Broad beans should be planted in a double row 20cm/8in apart with 15cm/6in between plants. This is slightly closer than they might be outdoors, but it seems to suit the conditions in a polytunnel.

Planting broad beans

If the soil is acid, scatter hydrated lime or wood ash along the row, taking care not to get any on the leaves of small plants. This will also help to keep any active slugs and snails at bay.

> ☑ Plant broad beans as close to a door as possible. This gives flowers the best chance of pollination in early spring. Peas are self-fertile and the first flowers don't need any help with pollination. They grow quite tall, however, so place them where they won't overshadow low-growing crops.

☑ If you decide that there isn't room in the polytunnel for a crop of broad beans, it's still worth raising young plants in pots from an autumn sowing. You can plant these out in the garden and they will often crop better than ones that are direct sown outdoors. Just make sure to cover the row with a cloche, so that they don't suffer too much of a shock in the move from the tunnel to the great outdoors.

Extra early potatoes

Some people get great results from planting first early potatoes in a polytunnel in December. This is only really an option for areas where a mild winter is the norm, but it can be worth having a go. Plant the sprouted seed potatoes 15cm/6in deep and 30cm/12in apart, in a soil enriched with plenty of compost. Nothing much will happen for a few weeks, but once the first shoots start to emerge keep a close eye on things. Always cover emerging leaves with extra layers of fleece – double or triple thickness may be required. If nights are really cold, cover each plant with a cardboard box. If days are cold as well, place a large clear plastic tub over every plant. Light levels might be reduced slightly, but this is less of a problem than frozen foliage. Potato leaves will discolour if they are lightly frosted, but a hard freeze can kill the growing plants outright. Adequate covering should avoid this problem and the reward will be an extra early crop next spring.

Carrots

If you sowed carrots in a pot in October or November, these should be well up by now. Don't thin the seedlings, even if they seem crowded. Slugs will eat some, some may just wilt, but the survivors will grow to cram the pot with tasty little roots.

Kohl rabi

Seed sown in late October will have produced small seedlings. These will be ready for planting out now. Growth can be very slow during the winter, but it is still worth getting small plants into the border: they will have a chance to become established before putting on growth next year.

Tomatoes and peppers

All the other summer crops will be long gone, but in a good year a few tomatoes and peppers can hang on until December in an unheated polytunnel. It might even be possible to pick the last cherry tomatoes for Christmas dinner, but it isn't really worth hanging on to diseased plants just for a handful of fruit.

'Bendigo' peppers still ripening

It's best to clear any remaining tomato and pepper plants in early December, especially if they have been grown in the border. This gives the soil a chance to recover before you plant out another year's tomatoes and peppers. Pick any ripe and unripe fruit and spread this out on a sunny window ledge. Be scrupulous about removing any fallen leaves and fruit. Dig lots of good compost into the empty bed and keep this damp so that microbes can do their work – the border should be healthy and ready for planting in the spring.

☑ Try not to pass any problems on to the next generation: plan to grow next year's tomato crop in a different part of the polytunnel.

Remove last
leaves from a
grape vine

Grape vines

Clear all fallen leaves from vines and pick free any leaves that haven't fallen. Some may stick against the polythene. Check the vine at the same time and cut away any diseased or damaged sections. Prune this year's side shoots back to leave one fat bud. Fruit will form next year on the new growth. Vines can take quite a hard pruning and they will bounce back with vigour next year.

Some people prefer to untie vines from supports and to lay them down on the ground for the winter. This can be fiddly, if not extremely difficult, to do. Provided the vine is held away from the polythene, and provided you check it over and prune it back, it doesn't have to be moved.

Look after the structure

This may seem repetitive, but if you maintain the structure of the polytunnel well it will last for years. The winter months usually see most damage, so repetitive checks and repairs are just the thing (see Part 6).

- Check all polythene regularly, especially at corners and where it crosses the framework. Repair any rips before they spread.
- Check catches and hinges on doors, so that these don't break off and flap loose in a winter storm.
- If an elderly polytunnel has wooden door frames which go down into the ground, check that these haven't rotted through over the years. For a quick repair, knock a strong post in and fix the old frame to this.

☑ If the structure suffers from prevailing winds that blow directly in through the door, it may be worth rehanging the door from the other side of the frame.

Order seeds

Early December is a good time to send off for seed catalogues. Get a few, as this will give a wider choice. Once someone is on the distribution list, companies usually send catalogues out automatically in subsequent years.

It's worth taking the time to sit down and work out what to grow next year: what to buy as plants and what to grow from seed. Consider factors like disease resistance, vigour and size. This should be a pleasant job, so don't rush! Ideally, seed orders should be sent off before the end of the year. This gives you the best choice of varieties – some may sell out if you leave ordering too late – but in practice, in January you will still be in plenty of time to get your order in.

Extra fittings?

December is a quiet time to review the polytunnel and assess what might be useful in the year ahead. Is there enough bench space? Would shelves be useful, or would they get in the way? What about a watering system? Or soil-warming cables? Then there are paths and raised beds . . .

Don't rush into making expensive decisions, but do look into anything that might make the workload easier.

Remember that:
- Shelves can be hung from the polytunnel framework.
- It's a good idea to dig out paths and add the extra topsoil to the borders. Back sufferers will appreciate the raised beds.
- Soil won't fall on to paths if it is held back behind planks of wood.
- A board across a couple of boxes, or bins, makes a quick bench that can be moved as needed.

Wash those dirty pots!
A year's worth of sowing and potting on will leave behind a pile of dirty pots. To minimize the possibility of disease being carried through to next year's sowings, all tubs, trays and pots should be washed. Some people are organized enough to scrub each pot as it empties and, since damp compost lifts off the inside of a pot much more easily than compost that has been left to dry on for several months, this is the ideal thing to do. More people make a pile of dirty pots and vow they will deal with them at a later time. Look on December as that time arriving! Fill a large bucket, or even a wheelbarrow, with warm water and an environmentally friendly washing liquid. Add some algae remover, or Citrox, or tea tree oil. Then find a nice sunny spot in the garden, sit down and start to scrub. A washing-up brush works well for getting into the corners and removing all debris.

Hanging shelves

Spread the washed pots out on the ground and hose them off with clean water. Once they are dry pots can be stacked and stored in boxes. They will be clean, disease and pest free, and all ready for the growing year to come.

Soil health
Gardeners expect a lot from the patch of earth inside a polytunnel. It gets little rest and is often expected to crop on a year-round basis. This may work out extremely well for the first year, but fertility will decrease and pest and disease problems increase over subsequent years, unless you take some action. Some people choose to grow only in growbags and containers, so that the compost can be changed with each crop. Others dig out and replace the border soil every few years, which seems like an awful lot of work. The best option is to look after the beds that are there and keep them in good condition so that they can crop well without any change of soil (see Part 6).

Break up any green crust that forms on the soil

December is the perfect time to get things sorted. Clear any debris and remove any diseased material before adding anything that might cover the problem up. Borders in a polytunnel can become covered in a green crust during the winter months; this is most common on wet heavy soil. Riffle around plants, with gloved fingers or a hoe, to break up the surface and help the soil to 'breathe'.

Adding well-made compost can restore vigour to old beds and will often help sort out disease problems too. A layer of seaweed, applied as mulch in December, can work wonders. Well-rotted manure will replace lost nutrients and the border will be all ready for planting out in the spring.

☑ Pile fresh manure in a corner of the polytunnel. It will generate heat as it rots and, after this process is finished, it can be spread around over the soil.

Enjoy the December harvest

Last peppers	Spinach
Last tomatoes	Chard
Salad leaves	Kohl rabi
Lettuce	Potatoes
Fennel	Kale
Beetroot	Pak choi
Turnip	Swiss chard
Oriental greens	

Some harvesting hints

- Harvest cut-and-come-again crops regularly to keep them producing and preferably pick while the taste is still sweet.
- **Winter lettuce, mibuna, mizuna, land cress, lamb's lettuce, mustard greens, rocket, purslane,** etc., can all provide plenty of picking for winter salads.
- If you sowed **pak choi** in August, it can stand well into December, but not much longer, so pick and use plants now.
- Make sure you lift any late-cropping **potatoes** and get all small tubers out of the ground. The earliest new potatoes can be planted this month and it's not worth risking the spread of disease to next year's crop.
- **Fennel** bulbs may not reach the size of summer ones, but they taste wonderful when picked fresh in December, as do small tasty beetroot and spinach leaves.
- Keep harvesting and be patient: small things will come into their own as the days start to lengthen again.

RIGHT: Florence
fennel
OPPOSITE:
December harvest

4

FRUIT AND VEGETABLES AT A GLANCE

AUBERGINES

AUBERGINES	Jan	Feb	Mar	Apr	May	Jun	Jul	Aug	Sep	Oct	Nov	Dec
Sow	░	░	░									
Plant					▓	▓						
Harvest							▓	▓	▓	▓		

January	Buy seed. Choose an early variety. Sow a few seed in an 8cm/3in pot. Cover with 6mm compost. Put in a plastic bag and keep at 20–25°C/68–77°F. Germination can take 7–21 days.
February	Prick seedlings out into individual 8cm/3in pots. Keep at 20°C/68°F.
March	Keep seedlings warm, watered and growing steadily.
April	Pot on into 12cm/5in pots if necessary. Give plants a health check. Watch out for greenfly. Buy in plants if you haven't sown seed.
May	Harden plants off. Plant out in late May if nights are above 12–15°C/54–59°F. Provide an extra cloche or fleece cover to keep plants warm.
June	Plant out later sowings: two plants per growbag, one plant per 30cm/12in pot or in the border soil 45cm/18in apart. First flowers may need a hand with pollination.
July	Pollinate flowers with a paintbrush. Spray overhead if the weather is hot and dry. Watch out for red spider mite. Start feeding plants in pots by the end of the month. Feed every ten days while fruit is swelling. Keep soil damp.
August	Use aluminium foil to reflect light, if sunshine levels are low. Harvest first ripe fruit – watch out for spines.
September	Harvest lots of ripe fruit while it is firm. Watch out for aphids and for slugs nibbling fruit. Remove any plants that show no sign of fruiting. Reduce watering.
October	Pick any last fruit and remove all plants and fallen leaves.
November	
December	Buy seed.

AUBERGINE TROUBLES	Jan	Feb	Mar	Apr	May	Jun	Jul	Aug	Sep	Oct	Nov	Dec
Slugs			░	░	░	░	░	░				
Red spider mite					▓	▓	▓	▓	▓			
Whitefly				░	░	░	░	░	░	░		
Aphids			▒	▒	▒	▒	▒	▒	▒	▒		
Grey mould			▓	▓	▓	▓	▓	▓	▓	▓		
Dry set					░	░	░					

BASIL

BASIL	Jan	Feb	Mar	Apr	May	Jun	Jul	Aug	Sep	Oct	Nov	Dec
Sow												
Plant												
Harvest												

January	Buy seed.
February	Be patient and don't sow until next month.
March	Sow three or four seeds per cell or small pot. Barely cover with compost. Cover with polythene or a plastic lid, and leave on a sunny window ledge in the house. Germination takes 5–7 days.
April	Keep compost damp but not soggy. Leave seedlings on the window ledge. Make a second sowing of seed.
May	Plant out March sowings as soon as the last frost has passed. Basil likes to get roots down into a damp (not wet) soil enriched with compost. Plant clumps of three seedlings 30cm/12in apart. Make a final sowing of seed – try growing some in a large pot.
June	Start picking leaves. Pinch out whole clusters from the top of stems before they flower. More leaves will grow from leaf joints lower down the stem.
July	Basil is at its best for the next two months. Pick regularly and always nip out flower spikes. Water so that the ground is damp – not too wet or too dry.
August	Keep harvesting as for July. Make pesto.
September	Strip any green leaves from failing plants and remove them. The whole patch doesn't have to clear at the same time. An early frost will blacken leaves. Cover with fleece to try to prolong the harvest. Bring a healthy potted plant indoors to grow on.
October	Harvest any remaining leaves before they blacken. Remove plants.
November	
December	

BASIL TROUBLES	Jan	Feb	Mar	Apr	May	Jun	Jul	Aug	Sep	Oct	Nov	Dec
Slugs												
Aphids												
Caterpillars												
Grey mould												

BEETROOT

BEETROOT	Jan	Feb	Mar	Apr	May	Jun	Jul	Aug	Sep	Oct	Nov	Dec
Sow		▓	▓			▓						
Plant			▓	▓			▓	▓	▓			
Harvest	▓	▓	▓	▓	▓	▓	▓					▓

January	Harvest beetroot if they are golf-ball size or larger. Harvest a few fresh leaves from each plant if other crops are in short supply; don't take too many, as this will stop roots swelling.
February	Make sowings in cells for the earliest outdoor crops. Keep an eye on overwintered plants. Remove any discoloured leaves. Harvest roots before they become woody.
March	If the polytunnel is big enough, plant a few seedlings out from the Feb sowing. The rest can go outdoors, but a few plants in the tunnel will give earlier and sweeter crops. Soil should be enriched with compost. Plant 12cm/5in apart.
April	Keep harvesting either roots or a few leaves while small and sweet. Remove plants if they start to bolt, or when space is needed for other crops.
May	Harvest as necessary.
June	Make the first sowing of beetroot in cells for late autumn/early winter crops. If temperatures are high in the polytunnel, germinate seed somewhere cooler. Make sure the cells don't dry out.
July	A sowing made now will crop in late winter or early spring.
August	Sow at the beginning of the month for a late spring crop. First sowings can be planted out now. Allow 12cm/5in between plants – closer spacing can make them prone to leaf spot.
September	Try planting out in a hotbed after cucumbers have been removed. This gives plants a fast start so that more leaf is grown before the winter.
October	Keep plants watered and don't let the soil dry out.
November	Remove any discoloured leaves.
December	Watch out for grey mould. Remove discoloured leaves – more will grow.

BEETROOT TROUBLES	Jan	Feb	Mar	Apr	May	Jun	Jul	Aug	Sep	Oct	Nov	Dec
Slugs			▓	▓		▓	▓	▓	▓	▓		
Leaf spot	▓	▓									▓	▓
Damping off		▓	▓			▓	▓	▓	▓			

BROAD BEANS (EARLY CROP)

BROAD BEANS	Jan	Feb	Mar	Apr	May	Jun	Jul	Aug	Sep	Oct	Nov	Dec
Sow											░	░
Plant	■											■
Harvest				■	■							

January	Buy seed of overwintering varieties, so that there is plenty to last for autumn sowing. Plant out any sowings left in pots from last year (see Dec).
February	Put sticks at each end of the row and stretch string between these along each side of the row. This will stop plants from flopping. Protect small plants from slugs.
March	Keep watering as needed. The soil round roots should never be dry. Keep adding a row of string every 20cm/8in to support plants. First flowers should appear by the end of the month.
April	Plants will be full of flowers. These are self-fertile but may need some help. Leave doors open so that bees can find their way in. Water well while plants are flowering. First pods should be ready to pick this month.
May	Plants will crop well into May. Harvest pods while beans are young and tasty. Remove plants when space is needed for other crops, or when outdoor ones take over.
June	
July	
August	
September	
October	
November	Sow seed singly in 8cm/3in pots. Cover with polythene, but don't use any added heat. Alternatively, seed can go straight into the ground at spacings as for Dec, but always sow a few in pots to fill gaps. Watch out for rodents digging up and eating the seed.
December	Sow seed if not done in Nov. Plant out seedlings when 8cm/3in tall. Choose a planting spot close to a door. Dig a trench and fill with compost, topped with soil. Add lime if soil is acid. Plant beans in a double row, allowing 20cm/8in between the two rows and 15cm/6in between plants. Keep a few spare plants in pots to replace any gaps where plants fail in the row. Watch out for grey mould on seedlings in pots. If temperatures are low keep the row covered with fleece. Leaves might blacken a little in prolonged temperatures below 0°C/32°F, but the plant will grow more green leaves when things warm up.

BROAD BEAN TROUBLES	Jan	Feb	Mar	Apr	May	Jun	Jul	Aug	Sep	Oct	Nov	Dec
Slugs	░										░	░
Rats and mice	■										■	■
Grey mould	▓	▓									▓	▓

BROCCOLI

BROCCOLI	Jan	Feb	Mar	Apr	May	Jun	Jul	Aug	Sep	Oct	Nov	Dec
Sow				▦	▦	▦	▦					
Hold in pots					▦	▦	▦	▦				
Plant								▦	▦			
Harvest	▦	▦	▦	▦						▦	▦	▦

January	Start harvesting sprouting broccoli and any remaining calabrese.
February	Keep harvesting. Let the central spike grow large before cutting and never strip a plant.
March	Keep harvesting.
April	Sow purple sprouting varieties in trays or pots. Keep harvesting broccoli from plants sown last year. Clear plants that have finished cropping.
May	Prick out seedlings into deep tubs or 12cm/5in pots. Clear plants that have finished cropping.
June	Sow calabrese and sprouting varieties in trays or pots. Early sowings might need potting on to larger holding pots if there isn't space to plant out.
July	Make last sowings of sprouting broccoli. Watch out for slug damage to all seedlings and young plants.
August	Plant out into a part of the tunnel that was manured for a previous crop. Add lime if soil is acid. Allow 45cm/18in between plants and 60cm/24in between rows. Make last sowings of calabrese.
September	Keep an eye out for caterpillars. Keep plants watered and provide stakes to tie plants in as they grow.
October	Harvest calabrese as soon as decent heads form.
November	Keep harvesting calabrese.
December	Keep harvesting. Watch out for aphids in the folds of leaves. Grey mould can be a problem in the winter months.

BROCCOLI TROUBLES	Jan	Feb	Mar	Apr	May	Jun	Jul	Aug	Sep	Oct	Nov	Dec
Slugs	▦	▦	▦						▦	▦	▦	▦
Aphids	▦	▦	▦	▦						▦	▦	▦
Grey mould	▦	▦	▦							▦	▦	▦
Caterpillars								▦	▦			

CABBAGE (SPRING)

SPRING CABBAGE	Jan	Feb	Mar	Apr	May	Jun	Jul	Aug	Sep	Oct	Nov	Dec
Sow							▒	▒	▒			
Plant								▓	▓	▓	▓	
Harvest		▓	▓	▓	▓							

January	Give overwintered plants a liquid feed.
February	New soft growth will start as soon as temperatures rise. Watch out for slugs hidden between leaves. Harvest first plants while small, if you have grown plenty.
March	July-sown plants will be ready to harvest. Use them over the next few weeks.
April	August-sown plants will be ready to harvest.
May	September-sown plants will be ready to harvest.
June	
July	Make the first sowing. Sow in pots or trays and cover with compost. If temperatures are too high in the polytunnel, find a cooler place. Germination should take 5–7 days.
August	Prick seedlings out into deep tubs or larger pots if there is no space free in which to plant out. Plants should go into the border soil when 15cm/6in tall. They can follow on from a previously manured crop. Allow 45cm/18in between plants. Add lime if soil is acid. Make a second sowing for later spring greens.
September	Make a last sowing in early September. Keep planting out earlier sowings. Watch out for caterpillars, which can destroy young plants.
October	Spread the contents of the cucumber hotbed around growing cabbages. Watch out for signs of clubroot disease if buying in plants.
November	Young plants will be established. They need little attention other than the occasional watering if the soil dries out.
December	As for November.

SPRING CABBAGE TROUBLES	Jan	Feb	Mar	Apr	May	Jun	Jul	Aug	Sep	Oct	Nov	Dec
Slugs	▒	▒	▒	▒			▒	▒	▒	▒	▒	▒
Aphids	▒	▒	▒	▒	▒	▒	▒	▒	▒	▒	▒	▒
Grey mould	▓	▓	▓		▓				▓	▓	▓	▓
Caterpillars								▒	▒			
Damping off							▓	▓	▓			

CARROTS (EARLY CROP)

CARROTS	Jan	Feb	Mar	Apr	May	Jun	Jul	Aug	Sep	Oct	Nov	Dec
Sow	▨	▨								▨	▨	
Harvest				▨	▨							

January	Sow early short-rooted varieties like 'Amsterdam Forcing' and 'Early Nantes' in 30cm/12in pots of good compost. Sow direct in drills filled with compost in the border, but don't add any manure. Allow 20cm/8in between rows. Cover with layers of fleece for extra protection. Wait until Feb if the weather is cold. Germination can take 14–21 days, but can be longer at low temperatures.
February	Sow in pots, or in the border, as for Jan.
March	Protect against slugs as seedlings emerge and until they are 10cm/4in tall. Keep covered with fleece until plants are tall and growing well. Water if soil starts to dry out.
April	Keep compost damp but not soggy. Plants in pots will be crowded, but don't thin: this will give a crop of fingerling roots. First baby roots might be ready for eating from autumn sowings.
May	Harvest roots as needed. Carrot fly shouldn't be a problem with early crops in the polytunnel.
June	All roots should be cleared by June.
July	
August	
September	
October	Sow seed, as for Jan, in mild areas.
November	Sow seed in mild areas.
December	

CARROT TROUBLES	Jan	Feb	Mar	Apr	May	Jun	Jul	Aug	Sep	Oct	Nov	Dec
Slugs		▨	▨	▨							▨	▨
Damping off	�as	▨									▨	▨

COURGETTES

COURGETTES	Jan	Feb	Mar	Apr	May	Jun	Jul	Aug	Sep	Oct	Nov	Dec
Sow		▓	▓									
Plant				▓	▓							
Harvest					▓	▓	▓	▓	▓	▓	▓	

January	Buy seed.
February	In warmer areas, try sowing a couple of seeds of the variety 'Parthenon' at the end of the month. Keep these on a sunny window ledge.
March	Make a first sowing at the beginning of March and another one at the end of the month. Try different varieties, such as 'Dundoo', 'Defender' or 'Venus', for compact plants. Sow one seed per 8cm/3in pot and cover with a plastic bag. Keep at 20°C/68°F. Seed takes 6–8 days to germinate.
April	Pot on into 12cm/5in pots if necessary. Harden off and plant out at the end of the month. Fill a hole with compost and plant the courgette on top. Allow 60cm/24in between plants. Mark the planting point with a stick so that it is easy to know where to water when the ground is covered with large leaves. Cover with a large clear plastic tub, or cloche, to give extra protection on cold nights.
May	Harvest first fruit while small. Keep plants covered on cold nights, but don't restrict growth. Water well – courgettes are thirsty plants.
June	Watch out for powdery mildew. Keep soil moist. Keep harvesting small fruits. Look under leaves for ones that have turned into marrows.
July	If outdoor plants are growing well, remove most, or all, of the polytunnel ones. Leave one or two if you want to extend the season in autumn.
August	Cut back foliage if it's spreading too much. Keep an eye out for powdery mildew and water well. Pick all fruit as it comes ready and don't leave marrows to ripen on the plant.
September	Courgette production slows down over the next weeks. Keep harvesting. Even if plants look tatty they will still produce. Watch out for roots rotting in cold wet soil.
October	Plants will die after a night of hard frost. Evict them once fruit stops growing.
November	In a mild year, the last courgettes can be harvested in November from a spring sowing.
December	Buy seed.

COURGETTE TROUBLES	Jan	Feb	Mar	Apr	May	Jun	Jul	Aug	Sep	Oct	Nov	Dec
Slugs			▓	▓								
Powdery mildew					▓	▓	▓	▓	▓	▓		
Grey mould					▓	▓	▓	▓	▓	▓	▓	
Root rot									▓	▓	▓	

CUCUMBERS

CUCUMBERS	Jan	Feb	Mar	Apr	May	Jun	Jul	Aug	Sep	Oct	Nov	Dec
Sow			▓	▓	▓	▓	▓					
Plant					▓	▓	▓					
Harvest					▓	▓	▓	▓	▓	▓		

January	
February	Be patient and don't sow until next month.
March	Sow seed singly, 1cm/½in deep, in 8cm/3in pots. Cover with a polythene bag. Keep at 20°C/68°F. Don't exclude light. Germination takes 5–7 days.
April	Pot on into 12cm/5in pots. Water very carefully and keep plants above 15°C/59°F but below 30°C/86°F. Make a second sowing of seed.
May	Plant out 45cm/18in apart in a hotbed, or on a mound of soil, once temperatures settle and frost is passed. Slit the bottom of growbags before putting two cucumber plants in each of these. Watch out for root rot if large plants are still in pots. Watch out for red spider mite and powdery mildew from now on. Pick the first fruit from early plants.
June	Plant out April sowings. Remove male flowers if the variety demands it. Train stems up strings. Harvest fruit before it becomes too large. Water carefully and spray overhead in dry weather. Pile fresh compost around the lower part of the stem.
July	Add more compost round the base of the stem. Train plants up to the roof and tie them in. Keep spraying overhead in hot weather. Harvest all ripe fruit even if there is a glut.
August	Nip the tops off plants, or turn them round and grow them back down to the ground again. Use a liquid feed every ten days and add more compost round the stem. Water carefully and spray twice a day if hot.
September	Remove any discoloured leaves and failing fruit. Keep applying liquid feed. Remove any plants that stop producing, or that start to die back.
October	Harvest any remaining fruit and remove plants.
November	
December	

CUCUMBER TROUBLES	Jan	Feb	Mar	Apr	May	Jun	Jul	Aug	Sep	Oct	Nov	Dec
Slugs			▓	▓	▓							
Red spider mite					▓	▓	▓	▓	▓			
Whitefly				▓	▓	▓	▓	▓	▓	▓		
Aphids			▓	▓	▓	▓	▓	▓	▓	▓		
Powdery mildew					▓	▓	▓	▓	▓	▓		
Gummosis				▓	▓	▓	▓	▓	▓			
Grey mould			▓	▓	▓	▓	▓	▓	▓	▓		
Root rot				▓	▓	▓	▓					

FIGS

FIGS	Jan	Feb	Mar	Apr	May	Jun	Jul	Aug	Sep	Oct	Nov	Dec
Plant												
Harvest												

January	Pot-grown figs can be planted at any time of year. Protect plants with a layer of fleece in cold winters to prevent fruit drop.
February	Try planting a 'Brown Turkey' or 'Brunswick' fig in a 38cm/15in pot. Established bushes should have small fruitlets, formed last autumn, in the leaf joints.
March	March and April are good months for planting figs. These can go straight into the soil of a large polytunnel. Roots should be confined so that bushes produce fruit rather than leaf. Dig a large hole (1m/39in square and 50cm/20in deep) and line it with bricks or concrete, or use a large container. Fill with a compost and soil mix – this shouldn't be too rich and aim for pH 6.5. Fruit may not be produced for two or three years. Prune overcrowded and crossed branches in early March.
April	Leaves will start to grow. Small figlets, formed last autumn, will start to swell. Keep compost moist, especially on newly planted trees.
May	Water daily in hot weather and mist over leaves. Fruit should be swelling steadily. Remove any small and discoloured fruit. Use a mulch to keep moisture in the soil.
June	Keep watering and misting in hot weather. Remove any split fruit. Don't feed unless the tree is bearing a large crop.
July	First fruit will ripen at the end of a sunny month. The skin changes colour and the neck flops. Ripe figs feel just soft when pressed. Stop spraying leaves with water when fruit is ripening.
August	Use netting or fleece to keep birds and wasps from spoiling ripe fruit. Harvest fruit when ripe and before it splits. Use soon after picking. Small figlets will start to grow in the leaf joints near the top of shoots: these will form the next year's crop. If bushes are to be kept small, nip the tops off all shoots that have finished cropping – don't remove figlets in doing so.
September	Bushes will finish fruiting. Keep an eye on small figlets. Remove any that are larger than a pea. These would have formed a second crop in a warm climate, but they will be too big to survive the winter.
October	Keep removing any figlets larger than a pea in size.
November	Cut out any dead or damaged wood. Clear fallen leaves.
December	Cover bushes with fleece if the winter is very cold.

FIG TROUBLES	Jan	Feb	Mar	Apr	May	Jun	Jul	Aug	Sep	Oct	Nov	Dec
Grey mould												
Birds												
Wasps												

FLORENCE FENNEL
(AS AN OVERWINTER CROP)

FENNEL	Jan	Feb	Mar	Apr	May	Jun	Jul	Aug	Sep	Oct	Nov	Dec
Sow						▓	▓	▓	▓			
Plant							▓	▓	▓	▓		
Harvest	▓	▓	▓	▓	▓						▓	▓

January	Harvest as needed. Keep covered with fleece if temperatures are below 0°C/32°F.
February	Harvest as needed.
March	Buy seeds. Harvest as needed.
April	Harvest before plants bolt. (Seed can be sown now for a summer crop.)
May	Lift any remaining plants.
June	Sow seed thinly in deep pots or trays. Keep at 15–20°C/59–68°F until germinated.
July	A good time to sow seed. Don't let seedlings overheat and don't overwater.
August	Sow seed. Plant seedlings out when they are 10cm/4in tall. Border soil should be enriched with compost. Keep roots intact. Water well and protect against slugs. If there is no space available, pot on into deeper containers until ready to plant out.
September	Sow seed. Plant out 20cm/8in apart in rows 30cm/12in apart.
October	Get all plants into the soil by the end of the month, however small.
November	Plants will grow steadily and bulbs will swell. Harvest when full and firm.
December	Harvest as needed. Cover with fleece if nights are cold.

FENNEL TROUBLES	Jan	Feb	Mar	Apr	May	Jun	Jul	Aug	Sep	Oct	Nov	Dec
Slugs						▓	▓	▓				
Grey mould	▓	▓	▓								▓	▓
Damping off						▓	▓	▓				

FRENCH BEANS

FRENCH BEANS	Jan	Feb	Mar	Apr	May	Jun	Jul	Aug	Sep	Oct	Nov	Dec
Sow			▓	▓	▓	▓	▓	▓				
Plant				▓	▓	▓	▓	▓				
Harvest					▓	▓	▓	▓	▓	▓		

January	Buy seed.
February	
March	Sow dwarf French beans singly, 1cm/½in deep, in 5cm/2in cells, pots or tubs. Cover with a polythene bag. Keep at 15°C/59°F. Don't exclude light. Germination takes 5–7 days.
April	Plant out March sowings when plants have two proper leaves – around the middle of April. Plant in a double row over a trench filled with compost. Allow 20cm/8in between rows and 15cm/6in between plants. Scatter lime or wood ash if soil is acid. Cover with a double layer of fleece on cold nights. Sow seed of climbing varieties in 8cm/3in pots.
May	Harvest first small dwarf French beans from earliest sowings. Sow more seed for continuous crops. Plant out, or sow, climbing varieties. Plant over a trench of compost, 20cm/8in apart in a single row. Lime if necessary on acid soil. Provide a string for each plant to grow up.
June	There should be plenty of beans to harvest – look under leaves for hidden bunches. Keep soil damp. Watch out for red spider mite. Spray over leaves in hot weather. Sow climbing and dwarf varieties where they are to grow. Twine stems around strings to start them climbing.
July	Climbing varieties might be up to the roof and starting to crop. Pick regularly while small and tender. Water well and regularly. Use a liquid feed every two weeks to keep climbing plants producing. Be vigilant for red spider mite and remove any badly affected dwarf plants. Remove plants that have finished cropping. Still time to sow dwarf varieties.
August	Watch out that climbing varieties don't shade crops that need sun.
September	Keep harvesting.
October	Harvest any remaining beans and shell the seeds if pods are tough.
November	
December	

FRENCH BEAN TROUBLES	Jan	Feb	Mar	Apr	May	Jun	Jul	Aug	Sep	Oct	Nov	Dec
Slugs			▓	▓	▓							
Red spider mite					▓	▓	▓	▓	▓	▓		
Aphids			▓	▓	▓	▓	▓	▓	▓	▓		
Grey mould			▓	▓	▓	▓	▓	▓	▓	▓		

GRAPES

GRAPES	Jan	Feb	Mar	Apr	May	Jun	Jul	Aug	Sep	Oct	Nov	Dec
Plant												
Harvest												

January	Pot-grown vines can be planted at any time of the year. Prune and tidy established vines, if you have not done so already, before they start into growth.
February	
March	Tie vines back on to support wires if taken down last year. Do this at the beginning of March before growth starts. Apply a thick layer of manure as a mulch around the stem.
April	Plants will start into growth. Nip out growing points on side shoots of new vines.
May	Small clusters of flowers start to form. Keep the vine under control. Train the main stem along the ridge of the polytunnel and tie it in as it grows. Water well around the roots and don't let the soil dry out.
June	Embryo fruit bunches start to swell. Keep watering daily, if needed, in dry weather. Start pruning. Established vines: stop any shoot that has formed two bunches of grapes two leaves after the second bunch. Stop shoots that haven't formed bunches after two or three leaves. Don't prune the main stem, but do continue to tie it in. New vines: don't allow these to fruit. Leave two main shoots to grow on (the strongest will be selected as the leader next year) and prune side shoots back after they have grown five leaves.
July	Keep watering daily in dry weather. Remove any poorly formed bunches (up to a half of all bunches). Keep pruning back growth on side shoots. Thin out the smallest grapes from dessert bunches, so that the rest grow well. Make sure light and air can reach around the growing bunches of grapes. Keep training new vines as above.
August	There should be lots of bunches of grapes all swelling nicely. Some might start to reach full colour and be sweet enough to eat at the end of the month. Watch out for grey mould and remove any affected bunches. Keep watering while fruit is swelling. Keep excess foliage under control.
September	Most bunches should ripen this month. Check to see how sweet grapes taste before picking a lot. Sun will make them sweeter. Watch out for grey mould, which can ruin the crop. Check the centre of bunches for hiding woodlice and earwigs. Net doors to keep birds away from the ripe crop.
October	Continue to harvest while grapes are sound and sweet tasting. Remove bunches that are past their best and pick up fallen fruit. Time to think about planting a bare-rooted vine.
November	Plant vines outside the polytunnel and train the stem in around the edge of the door frame. Dig a 45cm/18in-square hole and half fill this with compost. Fill with soil and plant the vine to the same level that it was grown before. Add lime to pH7 if necessary. Clear fallen leaves.
December	Still time to plant bare-rooted vines. Cut the main stem back to leave three or four strong buds after planting. Vines can be untied and laid on the ground. Remove remaining leaves. Prune this year's side shoots back to leave one fat bud.

GRAPE TROUBLES	Jan	Feb	Mar	Apr	May	Jun	Jul	Aug	Sep	Oct	Nov	Dec
Red spider mite												
Powdery mildew												
Woodlice/earwigs												
Grey mould												
Birds												

KOHL RABI

KOHL RABI	Jan	Feb	Mar	Apr	May	Jun	Jul	Aug	Sep	Oct	Nov	Dec
Sow												
Plant												
Harvest												

January	Buy seed. Choose a purple-skinned variety like 'Azur Star' or 'Kohlribi' and a green one like 'Noriko' or 'Olivia'.
February	Make the first sowings in a pot or tray. Cover with bubble wrap. Harvest plants sown last year – using those between golf-ball and tennis-ball size – but don't let plants go to seed.
March	Seed sown now will germinate in around seven days. Growth will be faster than for earlier sowings. Plant out when seedlings are 5cm/2in tall. Allow 25cm/10in between rows and 15cm/6in between plants.
April	You can sow seed over the next few months if this is a favourite crop, but kohl rabi grows well outdoors during the summer, so save the polytunnel for early and late crops. Keep harvesting. Remove any plants that bolt. Continue to plant out when 5cm/2in tall.
May	Keep plants watered well. Harvest roots while small and tender.
June	Keep harvesting. Clear any plants that bolt.
July	Make the first sowings in pots for autumn and winter crops.
August	Sow for winter crops. Plant out seedlings when 5cm/2in tall. Keep roots damp in hot weather. Watch out for caterpillars on the leaves.
September	Still time to make late sowings.
October	Make the last sowing of the year, if temperatures are above 5°C/41°F.
November	
December	Buy seed.

KOHL RABI TROUBLES	Jan	Feb	Mar	Apr	May	Jun	Jul	Aug	Sep	Oct	Nov	Dec
Slugs												
Caterpillars												
Damping off												

LETTUCE

LETTUCE	Jan	Feb	Mar	Apr	May	Jun	Jul	Aug	Sep	Oct	Nov	Dec
Sow	■	■	■	■	■	■	■	■	■	■	■	■
Plant	■	■	■	■	■	■	■	■	■	■	■	■
Harvest	■	■	■	■	■	■	■	■	■	■	■	■

January	Sow looseleaf, butterhead and cos varieties. Sow seed thinly in pots or trays and just cover with compost. Cover with polythene or bubble wrap until seed germinates. Harvest plants sown last autumn. Plant out seedlings sown last November. Allow 20cm/8in between rows and 20cm/8in between plants.
February	Sow spring and summer varieties in trays or pots. Harvest autumn-sown plants before leaves turn bitter.
March	Sow summer varieties with no added heat. Plant out seedlings sown in January. Put compost in the bottom of drills before planting. Always mark rows with sticks and string. Water after planting and protect from slugs. Watch out for cutworm eating through plants at ground level.
April	Continue to sow summer varieties in pots. Varieties to be used as small salad leaves can be sown *in situ*. Harvest November sowings. Plant out seedlings. Allow 30cm/12in between rows for summer varieties. Remove any bolted or bitter plants.
May	Keep sowing and planting out for a regular supply. Remove any bolted or bitter plants.
June	Keep sowing and planting out. Use plants while small and before they bolt. Remove a leaf or two at a time if preferred. Grow lettuce in the shade of taller plants through the summer months.
July	Make a last sowing of summer varieties, but also start sowing winter varieties.
August	Sow more winter lettuce varieties. Get seedlings into the ground as soon as space clears.
September	Sow more winter varieties if needed. These grow more slowly than summer crops, so may not be ready to use until the spring. Plant July and August sowings.
October	Sow in October for spring crops. Clear the last of the summer varieties. Get any seedlings into the ground even if small.
November	It's worth sowing in November if the month isn't too cold and if earlier sowings were missed. Plants won't be big enough to use until April or May.
December	Try sowing if there are no earlier plants. Seeds will germinate above 5°C/41°F.

LETTUCE TROUBLES	Jan	Feb	Mar	Apr	May	Jun	Jul	Aug	Sep	Oct	Nov	Dec
Slugs		■	■	■	■	■	■	■	■	■		
Aphids			■	■	■	■	■	■	■	■		
Grey mould	■	■								■	■	■
Damping off	■	■	■	■	■	■	■	■	■	■	■	■

MELONS

MELONS	Jan	Feb	Mar	Apr	May	Jun	Jul	Aug	Sep	Oct	Nov	Dec
Sow		■	■	■								
Plant					■	■	■					
Harvest							■	■	■			

January	Buy seed.
February	Make the first sowing if heat can be guaranteed.
March	Sow six seeds in a 12cm/5in pot. Cover with a polythene bag. Keep at 20–25°C/68–77°F. Don't exclude light. Germination takes 5–7 days. If seed cases stick, remove very carefully. Prick out and pot on seedlings from Feb sowings into individual 8cm/3in pots.
April	Keep plants above 15°C/59°F and don't overwater. Pot on as needed.
May	Plant out in the latter half of the month, but only if temperatures are reliably above 15°C/59°F. Always harden plants off first. Plant out 30cm/12in apart in a hotbed, or on a mound of soil, once temperatures settle and danger of frost has passed. Slit the bottom of growbags before putting two or three melon plants in each of these.
June	Most melons will be planted out in June, once temperatures are settled. Tie strings to the frame for support. Watch for first flowers – females have a small melon-shape swelling behind them. Use male flowers to pollinate if necessary. Water very carefully to avoid root rot. Spray leaves in hot weather.
July	Support fruit in nets so that stems don't break. Harvest first melons when ripe. Pile fresh compost around the base of the stem. Keep pollinating female flowers. Twirl stems round strings as they grow.
August	Keep stems tied in to strings if they don't twirl round naturally. Keep harvesting fruit when ripe and before it splits. Watch out for red spider mite. Spray overhead in hot weather.
September	Harvest any last fruit and remove plants.
October	
November	
December	

MELON TROUBLES	Jan	Feb	Mar	Apr	May	Jun	Jul	Aug	Sep	Oct	Nov	Dec
Slugs			■	■	■							
Red spider mite					■	■	■	■	■			
Whitefly				■	■	■	■	■	■	■		
Aphids			■	■	■	■	■	■	■	■		
Powdery mildew					■	■	■	■	■	■		
Gummosis				■	■	■	■	■	■	■		
Grey mould			■	■	■	■	■	■	■	■		
Root rot			■	■	■	■	■	■	■			

PEAS (MANGETOUT, AS A SPRING CROP)

MANGETOUT PEAS	Jan	Feb	Mar	Apr	May	Jun	Jul	Aug	Sep	Oct	Nov	Dec
Sow	▓									▓	▓	▓
Plant	▓											▓
Harvest				▓	▓							

January	Buy seed so that there is plenty to last for an autumn sowing. It's still worth making a late sowing in pots or in the border soil. Seedlings sown in early winter can be planted out in a trench filled with compost and covered with soil. Set a double row 12cm/5in apart with 5cm/2in between plants. If soil is acid, scatter lime or wood ash on the surface. Cover with a layer of fleece if the weather is cold.
February	Push small, twiggy sticks into the ground on either side of the row for support.
March	Keep watering as needed; the soil around roots should never be dry. Use larger branches, or pea netting, to support the growing peas. Don't let plants flop and break or trail on the ground.
April	Self-fertile flowers will set pods without any help. Water well while plants are flowering. First pods should be ready to pick this month.
May	Plants will crop abundantly. Keep harvesting while pods are flat and juicy. Add more supports if plants start to flop under their weight. Remove plants at the end of the month if space is needed for other crops.
June	Plants will still crop, but pods might become tougher. Shell any large peas from pods. Clear all remaining pods and remove plants.
July	
August	
September	
October	Sow seed in pots of compost: four seeds, at 1cm/½in depth, per 10cm/4in pot. Cover with fleece and leave in the unheated polytunnel to germinate.
November	Sow seed in cells, pots or tubs as for October.
December	Plant out seedlings when 8cm/3in tall, as for Jan. Sow seed if you have not already done so. Watch out for grey mould on seedlings.

MANGETOUT TROUBLES	Jan	Feb	Mar	Apr	May	Jun	Jul	Aug	Sep	Oct	Nov	Dec
Slugs	▓										▓	▓
Rats and mice	▓	▓									▓	▓
Grey mould	▓	▓									▓	▓

PEACHES & NECTARINES

PEACHES AND NECTARINES	Jan	Feb	Mar	Apr	May	Jun	Jul	Aug	Sep	Oct	Nov	Dec
Plant											██	██
Harvest							██	██	██			

January	Cover with a layer of fleece if really cold.
February	Learn the difference between buds. Fruit buds are round and plump; leaf buds are pointed. Keep ground weed free. Mulch around established trees with rotted manure or compost to provide nitrogen. Add a sprinkling of powdered seaweed for potash.
March	First flowers are self-fertile, but use a paintbrush to ensure that enough of them set fruit. In the first year after planting, rub off all fruit buds. In the second and third years after planting, allow a few buds to form fruit, and in the fourth year the tree can bear a full crop. Remove any crossing branches or any that are diseased.
April	Water regularly while fruit is swelling. Once flowering has finished spray over the leaves with water.
May	Feed with liquid seaweed while the fruit is swelling. Thin clusters to a single fruit.
June	Remove any deformed or discoloured fruit. Leave only the best to grow on.
July	Keep spraying over leaves with water until fruit starts to ripen. There should be some ripe fruit by the end of the month.
August	Ripe fruit is slightly soft when pressed, is well coloured and gives off an intoxicating scent. The fruit should lift from the stalk without any need for force.
September	Cut out side shoots after you have finished harvesting, but leave the new shoot, or a bud, at the base to grow as a replacement.
October	Clear any fallen leaves.
November	Plant new trees when branches are bare. Prepare a plot at least 120cm/4ft square and 60cm/24in deep. Dig in plenty of rotted manure or compost and use lime on the surface of the soil to adjust to a pH of 7.
December	Peaches and nectarines in the polytunnel should avoid peach leaf curl. If growing them near a door, try to keep this closed from November to April.

PEACH AND NECTARINE TROUBLES	Jan	Feb	Mar	Apr	May	Jun	Jul	Aug	Sep	Oct	Nov	Dec
Red spider mite					██	██	██	██	██			
Aphids			██	██	██	██	██	██	██	██		
Powdery mildew					██	██	██	██	██	██		
Wasps/ants/earwigs							██	██	██			
Birds												

PEPPERS

PEPPERS	Jan	Feb	Mar	Apr	May	Jun	Jul	Aug	Sep	Oct	Nov	Dec
Sow		▓	▓									
Plant					▓	▓						
Harvest	▓						▓	▓	▓	▓	▓	▓

January	Buy seed. In a mild winter, last year's plants might still be cropping.
February	Sow seed singly in small pots. Just cover with a scattering of compost. Put in a polythene bag and keep at 20–25°C/68–77°F. Seed takes 14–21 days to germinate, but can take longer.
March	Remove the plastic bag and grow on at 15–20°C/59–68°F. Pot on if necessary.
April	Pot on into 8cm/3in pots when seedlings have grown two true leaves.
May	Pot on into larger pots if plants outgrow existing pots. Watch out for curled leaves as a sign of greenfly. Start to harden plants off. Plant out in late May if night temperatures don't fall below 12°C/54°F. If it's cold, wait until June before planting out.
June	Plant two or three plants per growbag, or one per 30cm/12in pot. In the border plants should be 45–60cm/18–24in apart, depending on the size of the variety. Soil should have added compost and plenty of potash.
July	First flowers will form in July. These are self-fertile, but tap stems gently and mist with water in dry weather to aid fruit set. Use aluminium foil to reflect light.
August	Use a liquid feed every week while fruit is swelling. Support laden stems. First green peppers can be picked this month, but leave them on the plant to turn red.
September	Harvest ripe fruit. Use aluminium foil to reflect light if sunshine levels are low. Keep feeding and don't let the soil dry out. Watch out for slugs in fruit.
October	Bring a chilli pepper, in a pot, into the house before the first frost. Keep harvesting ripe fruits. Reduce watering and stop feeding.
November	Clear any fallen or discoloured foliage. Harvest ripe peppers. Clear any plants that have finished cropping.
December	Pick all remaining fruit and clear all plants and fallen leaves.

PEPPER TROUBLES	Jan	Feb	Mar	Apr	May	Jun	Jul	Aug	Sep	Oct	Nov	Dec
Slugs			▓	▓	▓	▓	▓	▓	▓			
Red spider mite					▓	▓	▓	▓	▓	▓		
Whitefly				▓	▓	▓	▓	▓	▓			
Aphids			▓	▓	▓	▓	▓	▓	▓	▓	▓	▓
Grey mould			▓	▓	▓	▓	▓	▓	▓	▓	▓	▓
Dry set					▓	▓						

NEW POTATOES

NEW POTATOES	Jan	Feb	Mar	Apr	May	Jun	Jul	Aug	Sep	Oct	Nov	Dec
Plant		███					███					███
Harvest				███							███	███

January	In mild areas only, plant early varieties in the border soil. Use a mulch if the weather is very cold. Seed potatoes should be sprouted before planting. Allow 30cm/12in between plants and the same between rows. Alternatively, plant two potatoes per bucket, half fill with compost and cover with fleece. Chit potatoes ready for planting next month.
February	Plant early varieties in buckets and containers so that they don't interfere with the planting of summer crops.
March	Earth up as stems grow. If cold weather persists, give extra protection to any exposed leaves. Keep containers and borders watered, but not too wet.
April	Start harvesting tubers from Dec and early Jan sowings. Start by reaching a hand down the side of a bucket and sneak out a few tubers while leaving the rest to grow on. By the end of the month, most of the crop will be lifted before tomatoes go out.
May	Clear any remaining tubers early in May and make sure no small ones are left in the soil.
June	
July	Plant second-cropping seed potatoes (or ones left from the spring) in containers outdoors. Bring containers into the polytunnel as soon as foliage appears.
August	Earth up as plants grow.
September	Make sure all containers are indoors before temperatures fall.
October	Cover with extra layers of fleece or bubble polythene, to keep plants growing.
November	Harvest lovely new potatoes, or leave them until next month.
December	Lift new potatoes for a celebratory dinner. Plant early varieties in mild areas for the earliest crop.

POTATO TROUBLES	Jan	Feb	Mar	Apr	May	Jun	Jul	Aug	Sep	Oct	Nov	Dec
Blight							███	███	███	███		
Slugs			░░░	░░░	░░░				░░░	░░░	░░░	░░░

PUMPKINS & SQUASH

PUMPKINS AND SQUASH	Jan	Feb	Mar	Apr	May	Jun	Jul	Aug	Sep	Oct	Nov	Dec
Sow				▓								
Plant					▓							
Harvest							▓	▓	▓	▓		

January	Buy seed. Try varieties of pumpkin and squash that don't do so well outdoors – 'Butternut Squash' and 'Uchiki Kuri' are two good ones.
February	
March	
April	Sow single seeds, 1cm/½in deep per 12cm/5in pot. Keep at 20°C/68°F. Germination takes 6–14 days.
May	Pot on into 12cm/5in pots if necessary. Plant out at the same time as sweetcorn – around the middle of the month. Dig a hole and fill with compost. Use a stick to mark the planting point. Plant at the same level as the plant was growing in the pot. Seed can be sown directly in a 30cm/12in square hole filled with compost.
June	Pumpkins are thirsty plants, so keep them watered. Use the stick to find the roots of the plant. Train stems to weave around the corn stalks. Watch out for powdery mildew. This is worst if soil is dry.
July	Introduce a male flower spike into female flowers to aid early fruit set. Keep pollen dry. Several fruits should set on each plant. Keep watering and these will swell.
August	Put a board or slate under swelling pumpkins. This stops rot where they touch the ground. Trim back leaves, or train plants to grow out of an open door. First fruits will be ready to harvest.
September	Harvest all fruit when it stops swelling and has a good colour. Leave a length of stem attached. Pumpkins and squash can be left in the polytunnel until the first frost.
October	Harvest any remaining fruit and remove plants.
November	
December	

PUMPKIN TROUBLES	Jan	Feb	Mar	Apr	May	Jun	Jul	Aug	Sep	Oct	Nov	Dec
Slugs				▓	▓							
Powdery mildew					▓	▓	▓	▓	▓			
Grey mould						▓	▓	▓	▓	▓		
Root rot								▓	▓			

SALAD LEAVES (ROCKET, MIZUNA, ETC.)

SALAD LEAVES	Jan	Feb	Mar	Apr	May	Jun	Jul	Aug	Sep	Oct	Nov	Dec
Sow *in situ*												
Harvest												

January	Buy seed. Rocket and mizuna both do well from early sowings. Always sow *in situ*. Make a shallow trench 8cm/3in deep and fill this with compost before sowing in 1cm/½in-deep drills. Allow 30cm/12in between rows and scatter seed more thickly now than later in the year – a good pinch for every 25cm/10in of row.
February	Harvest overwintered leaves. Sow rocket etc. if you didn't do so in Jan.
March	Harvest regularly to stop plants going to seed. Sow a mix of leaves. Watch out for slugs.
April	Clear seeding crops. Start harvesting Jan sowings. Keep sowing for a fast turnover of small, sweet leaves. Lots of plants in the row means most grow well, even if a few are eaten or fail.
May	Keep rows well watered in hot weather. Watch out for greenfly. Keep sowing and harvesting. Always clear rows when leaves get too big – there will be more on the way. Sow mixtures with tender leaves, like basil, included.
June	Plants finish quickly in hot dry conditions, so water regularly to keep them cropping. New sowings will be up and ready to pick in around six weeks.
July	Start thinking about winter crops. Choose hardy mixtures and winter blends.
August	Short rows, sown every month, will give plenty to pick right through the winter.
September	Keep sowing as crops clear.
October	Harvest regularly, but don't strip whole rows if you intend them to crop through the winter.
November	Try sowing mizuna, rocket and mibuna in large pots.
December	Buy seed. Make sowings in pots that can be started off in a little heat before putting out in the polytunnel.

SALAD LEAF TROUBLES	Jan	Feb	Mar	Apr	May	Jun	Jul	Aug	Sep	Oct	Nov	Dec
Slugs												
Aphids												

SPINACH, SPINACH BEET & SWISS CHARD

SPINACH/CHARD	Jan	Feb	Mar	Apr	May	Jun	Jul	Aug	Sep	Oct	Nov	Dec
Sow		▓	▓	▓	▓	▓	▓	▓	▓	▓		
Plant			▓	▓	▓	▓	▓	▓	▓	▓	▓	▓
Harvest	▓	▓	▓	▓	▓	▓	▓	▓	▓	▓	▓	▓

January	Harvest overwintered crops. Remove leaves that are discoloured.
February	Keep harvesting. Make first sowings if temperatures aren't too low.
March	Sow spinach or spinach beet in pots or trays with no added heat. Cover with polythene.
April	Plant out seedlings when 3cm/1¼in tall. Put plenty of compost in the trench. Spinach beet will crop for months. Spinach can be sown *in situ*. Keep harvesting. Allow 30cm/12in between rows if thinning to single plants (20cm/8in apart). Allow 15cm/6in between rows if growing baby leaves.
May	Sow spinach *in situ*. Spinach beet can be sown in pots and planted out or sown direct in drills for small leaves. Water well – if it's too hot and dry, plants will bolt.
June	Continuous sowings can be made for use as baby leaves. Keep plants watered in dry weather so that they don't run to seed.
July	Sow Swiss chard 'Bright Lights' in pots for a winter and spring crop.
August	Still time to sow chard. Sow spinach and spinach beet now to crop right through the winter.
September	Sow winter varieties of spinach. Keep them well watered. Plant out chard, 20cm/8in apart in rows 30cm/12in apart. Dig compost into the ground or follow on from a well-fed crop.
October	Still time to sow spinach for a winter crop, but get it into the ground as soon as you can.
November	Harvest carefully and don't strip plants.
December	Buy seed. Harvest winter crops.

SPINACH/CHARD TROUBLES	Jan	Feb	Mar	Apr	May	Jun	Jul	Aug	Sep	Oct	Nov	Dec
Slugs			▓	▓	▓	▓	▓	▓	▓	▓		
Caterpillars							▓	▓	▓			
Leaf spot	▓	▓	▓	▓							▓	▓
Damping off		▓	▓						▓	▓		

STRAWBERRIES (EARLY)

STRAWBERRIES	Jan	Feb	Mar	Apr	May	Jun	Jul	Aug	Sep	Oct	Nov	Dec
Plant						███	███	███	███			
Harvest				███	███	███						

January	Give plants a health check and look in pots for vine weevil grubs. Bring pots back into the polytunnel and stand them on a layer of manure. Give plants very little water for two weeks until new growth starts.
February	Keep compost moist and don't let temperatures rise too high. Buy in strong young plants if you need more.
March	Early varieties might start to flower. Cover with fleece to protect flowers from frost.
April	Plants should be covered in flowers. Use a paintbrush to ensure even pollination. Keep compost damp and apply a liquid feed every seven days while fruit is swelling. In a warm spring there might be the first ripe fruit at the end of the month.
May	Cover with netting to keep birds off ripe fruit. Remove any fruit that is mouldy before the problem spreads. Keep feeding and water regularly while fruit is swelling. Pick all ripe fruit.
June	Keep harvesting. Watch out for slugs. Move pots out of the tunnel as soon as they stop producing fruit.
July	Peg runners down into 8cm/3in pots.
August	Continue to peg down runners, but only take the first young plant on any shoot. Remove any discoloured leaves from parent plants. Buy in more plants if needed.
September	Cut any shoot that joins parents to established, pegged-down plants. The new plants should have good roots by now and can be moved into 20cm/8in pots of compost. Remove any discoloured leaves. Pots should stay out of the polytunnel to be touched by frost.
October	If any flowers form, pick them off.
November	
December	In a very cold winter, bring pots back into the tunnel (see Jan).

STRAWBERRY TROUBLES	Jan	Feb	Mar	Apr	May	Jun	Jul	Aug	Sep	Oct	Nov	Dec
Slugs				███	███	███	███					
Red spider mite					███	███	███	███	███			
Whitefly			███	███	███	███						
Grey mould				███	███	███						
Vine weevil	███										███	███
Birds				███	███	███	███					

SWEETCORN

SWEETCORN	Jan	Feb	Mar	Apr	May	Jun	Jul	Aug	Sep	Oct	Nov	Dec
Sow				▓	▓	▓						
Plant				▓	▓	▓						
Harvest							▓	▓	▓	▓		

Month	
January	
February	
March	Buy seed, but don't choose more than one or two varieties.
April	Sow single seeds, 1cm/½in deep per 8cm/3in pot or root-trainer. Keep at 20°C/68°F. Germination takes 5–10 days. Keep above 12°C/54°F after that.
May	Plant out into the border soil when 10cm/4in high. Allow 30cm/12in between plants. Dig a hole and fill and refill with water. Allow to drain before filling with manure or compost and planting out corn. If using two varieties of corn allow three weeks between sowings.
June	Keep plants watered well. They should grow very fast. Sow more seed *in situ* for a chance at a late crop. Plant out May sowings.
July	Shake stems carefully, so that pollen falls from the male tassels, at the top of the plant, on to the female silks in the leaf joints. Hoe carefully between plants, so that brittle stems don't break (or grow a pumpkin to cover the ground in between).
August	Peel back leaves at the end of a corn cob. Press a kernel to check for ripeness. Pick eat and enjoy the ripe cobs. All cobs from one sowing usually ripen within a couple of weeks of one another.
September	Keep harvesting cobs from the later sowings. The season is short and these may not make full cobs. Remove plants once the crop is finished.
October	Harvest any remaining fruit and remove plants.
November	
December	

SWEETCORN TROUBLES	Jan	Feb	Mar	Apr	May	Jun	Jul	Aug	Sep	Oct	Nov	Dec
Damping off				▓	▓							
Rats							▓	▓	▓			

TOMATOES

TOMATOES	Jan	Feb	Mar	Apr	May	Jun	Jul	Aug	Sep	Oct	Nov	Dec
Sow		■	■	■								
Plant				■	■	■						
Harvest						■	■	■	■	■	■	■

January	Buy seed. Earliest sowings can be made with heat, but it is safest to wait.
February	Sow seed thinly and cover with a sprinkling of compost, water lightly and put the tray in a clear polythene bag. Keep between 15°C/59°F and 25°C/77°F. Don't exclude light. Germination takes 6–10 days. Remove the bag once seedlings appear.
March	Sow seeds as for Feb. Pot seedlings on into 8cm/3in pots. Maintain a temperature of around 18°C/64°F.
April	You can still sow seed, but you'll get faster crops if you buy in plants. Harden off before planting out at the end of the month (if above 10°C/50°F). Provide a potash-rich growing medium and canes or strings as support. Allow 45cm/18in between plants and 90cm/36in between rows.
May	Tie the stems in to the supports as the plants grow. Nip out side shoots in the joints between leaf and stem. Open doors on hot days. Water regularly and lightly mist first flowers.
June	Spray first trusses of flowers with a light mist of water to help fruit set. Keep nipping out side shoots and tie in stems every 15cm/6in. First green fruit should start to swell and ripen. Water regularly. Keep tunnel doors open if hot.
July	Watch out for disease. Remove any discoloured foliage. Keep the soil watered. Start feeding every week with a liquid feed. Pick tomatoes as they ripen. Start removing lower leaves.
August	Harvest regularly. Keep nipping out side shoots and check the base of the plant for unwanted new shoots. Feed plants every week and mist overhead if the polytunnel reaches high temperatures. Remove lower leaves to expose fruit to the sun.
September	Remove any blighted leaves and fruit before the problem spreads. Nip out the growing point if plants ramble too much, or leave it to grow for a crop of late fruit. Pick up any fallen fruit that may scatter seed on the ground.
October	Remove failing plants. Leave healthy plants to provide fruit for a few weeks yet. Remove leaves, so that stems are almost stripped and only the healthy top growth is left to feed the plant.
November	If leaves blacken, pick all fruit and clear plants out of the tunnel. Clear the ground of all dropped leaves and fruit – this avoids carrying disease into the next year's crop.
December	In a mild winter plants may slowly ripen fruit, but always clear them out of the tunnel before the end of the year.

TOMATO TROUBLES	Jan	Feb	Mar	Apr	May	Jun	Jul	Aug	Sep	Oct	Nov	Dec
Caterpillars							■	■	■			
Red spider mite					■	■	■	■				
Whitefly				■	■	■	■	■	■	■		
Aphids			■	■	■	■	■	■	■	■		
Leaf mould						■	■	■	■	■	■	
Blight						■	■	■	■	■	■	■
Grey mould						■	■	■	■	■	■	
Blossom end rot						■	■	■	■			
Greenback						■	■	■	■	■		
Dry set			■	■	■							

5

PESTS, DISEASES AND OTHER PROBLEMS – AN ORGANIC APPROACH

Polytunnel growing can be a mixed blessing when it comes to pests and diseases. It's easier to keep polytunnel crops isolated from all that threatens plants growing outdoors, but once something finds its way into a warm, humid, confined space, the rate of spread can be rapid indeed. The key to healthy crops is a healthy growing environment.

A few rules for healthy crops
- Keep your eyes open for any potential problem before it gets out of control.
- Keep the soil in good heart.
- Use organic techniques to regain some balance in the situation.
- Remove any foliage that is damaged by disease.
- Remove any affected plants if necessary.
- Make sure plants get enough water, but not too much.
- Make sure enough air can circulate around growing crops.
- Try to keep temperatures below 30°C/86°F.

It's possible that there will be no real problems in the first year of polytunnel growing, but these will build up over subsequent years. Every gardener has to cope with some pests and diseases at some point. Every gardener loses the odd plant, or has something that doesn't crop well. Don't panic! Lots of plants grow perfectly well while tolerating some level of disease or colony of pests. And a problem that raises its head one year may disappear for the next. Don't automatically reach for something poisonous to kill pests and diseases out of hand. Growing great crops is all about balance. If a spray kills a predator as well as a pest, a different pest, which the predator previously kept under control, might start to build up numbers instead.

Most problems have a solution and most solutions can be organic. Environmentally friendly options don't have to be less effective than any other kind. Work with the best that nature can offer and the rewards will be the best that nature can supply.

OPPOSITE: Cabbage white caterpillars
BELOW: Mealy aphids

SOME POLYTUNNEL PESTS

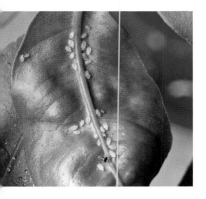

Greenfly

GREENFLY (aphids) can attack almost any plant, but their favourites are ones with plenty of soft new growth. Look on the underside of young leaves and around the growing points. Greenfly suck sap from the plant and to do this they aim for the easiest points. Viruses can be introduced directly by greenfly, or disease can get in through the wounds that they leave where they suck on sap. The first signs might be new leaves that are small and curled, or extended growing points with little sign of new leaf growth. If you leave greenfly unchecked, they can spill over on to flowers and fruit. Plants become sticky from the honeydew that the flies produce. This sweet substance is sought after by ants, which will guard colonies of greenfly from attack by predators.

What can you do about greenfly?
- If there are only one or two, squash them! Do this regularly until none are left.
- Spray with a jet of water aimed into troublespots. This will wash plenty of wingless females off the plant. Winged females could fly straight back, but repeat spraying will keep the problem under control. Plants in pots should be taken out of the polytunnel for spraying so that any squirted greenfly fall outdoors and won't so easily find their way back.
- Buy a biological control. *Aphidius* is a small black insect that kills greenfly. One insect can lay as many as 100 eggs. Each egg is laid into one immature aphid.
- Introduce ladybirds to eat the aphids. You can carry these into the tunnel from other parts of the garden or purchase them as larvae or adults.
- If legislation permits, sprays of soft soap and nettle tea are also effective controls.
- Plant nasturtiums to help keep greenfly away.

Blackfly

BLACKFLY are another type of aphid, but they don't attack such a wide range of plants. Look out for them around the tips of broad beans. The whole top of a plant may be smothered until stems look black. If left to their own devices, blackfly will spread down the stem and disfigure the whole plant, including pods. Attacks usually start in June, and the beans might well have finished cropping in the polytunnel then.

What can you do about blackfly?
• At the first signs of attack, simply cut off all growing points of all the plants, whether affected or not, since this is where blackfly always starts off. Either burn them or put the tops in a sealed polythene bag for a few weeks until all the flies are dispatched.

WHITEFLY isn't actually an aphid, although the two are related. Whiteflies also suck sap and produce honeydew, which encourages moulds. These small, waxy, white, winged insects can attack a wide range of polytunnel plants. Immature forms are green and scale-like, but these can also damage the growing plant. Strawberries, tomatoes and cucumbers can be particularly affected. If a cloud of white specks rises up in the air when you brush against a plant, check further. Turn a leaf over and look for the characteristic white insects. These are clear to spot against the green foliage.

What can you do about whitefly?
- If there are only one or two, squash them between your finger and thumb.
- Hang up sticky strips to trap flies. This may not control them, but it will indicate when they are present.
  Note: you must remove sticky traps before releasing any biological control.
- Use the biological control *Encarsia*.
- Plant a row of French marigolds to help repel whitefly.

RED SPIDER MITE can be a real problem in a hot, dry summer. These tiny mites look like minute crabs on the underside of leaves. Even though the name says 'red' they may well be green in the summer months. Leaves can start out with bleached spots but turn a mottled brownish-red in colour and there might be visible webs at the growing points. If you use a magnifying glass you can spot mites scuttling around the webs. Several plants can be attacked, but some seem to be favourites: aubergine, French bean, cucumber and melon are top of the list. If plants are severely affected, they will stop cropping.

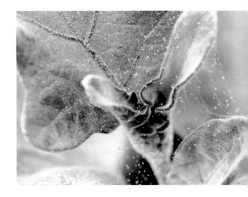

Red spider mite

What can you do about red spider mite?
- Spray overhead and keep everything damped down in hot weather. The mites don't like wet conditions.
- Use the biological control *Phytoseiulus*. This is a smaller mite, which feeds on the red spider ones.
- Scrub down frames, benches, etc. to destroy overwintering adults.

CATERPILLARS will happily munch their way through most leaves and fruit that they find themselves on. The adult butterflies and moths come in through open tunnel doors and look for the most appropriate place to lay their eggs. A tomato moth will choose a tomato plant, whereas a cabbage white butterfly will choose a brassica (even if it isn't totally specific as to which one). You may notice caterpillars in serious numbers around midsummer, but there will be far more in August and September. If there are large holes in leaves, look underneath and pay attention to any curls or folds in the foliage: caterpillars often hide in such places during the day. Droppings can be a telltale sign. These are dark, wet, and smell of boiled cabbage. Look out for rows of eggs glued to the underside of leaves. If these are dispatched before they hatch, damage can be avoided.

Caterpillar eggs stuck to a leaf

What can you do about caterpillars?
- Squash the eggs before they hatch.
- Hunt out the pests as soon as you notice damage. Pick off individual caterpillars and dispose of them (use tweezers or rubber gloves, because some caterpillars can cause a skin reaction).
- Cover low-growing crops with a fine mesh, so that butterflies can't get through to lay their eggs.
- Catch any butterflies and moths that find their way into the polytunnel. Pick them up and throw them out! They probably won't find their way back.
- Put screening material across the doors to allow air through but keep butterflies out.
- Use the biological control *Steinernema feltiae* directly on the caterpillars.

CUTWORMS, also called surface caterpillars, will eat through the stems of plants at ground level. Top of the list are lettuce. If a plant suddenly collapses in a row, check the stem. If it's cut through at ground level, a cutworm is almost certainly to blame. These pests feed at night and hide just under the surface of the soil during the day.

What can you do about cutworms?
- Dig around in the soil near where a plant has collapsed. The culprit is a greyish coloured grub about 4cm/1½in long. There is usually only one at a time, so dig it up and dispatch it.

TOP: Wireworms
BOTTOM: Slugs hide between leaves

WIREWORMS are most often a problem in newly cultivated soil and so may affect the polytunnel for the first couple of years after you put it up. The thin, segmented, orange-coloured larvae are up to 2cm/¾in long. They feed off grass roots if they hatch in a field, but if the field has been turned into a polytunnel border, they are happy to burrow into any root, bulb or stem that presents itself. The result can be a disheartening loss of a crop.

What can you do about wireworms?
- The problem decreases in subsequent years, so try sowing a sacrificial crop to get rid of most of the pests in one go. Potatoes are usually a favourite sacrificial crop. The tubers will be riddled with wireworm and may not be fit to eat, but the pests can be physically evicted along with the spuds.

SLUGS AND SNAILS must be some of the most annoying pests that a gardener faces. They creep out of hiding places when it turns dark and slither back at daybreak. In the meantime, they munch their way through pots of seedlings and eat holes in the leaves of larger plants. They can climb 2m/7ft up a climbing bean plant and hide in the leaves all day, just waiting to munch the beans at night. Not all varieties of slug are destructive and some eat only decaying vegetation, but nonetheless most gardeners have to use slug and snail controls.

What can you do about slugs and snails?

- Go out after dark with a torch and collect them up.
- Use organically approved slug pellets based on ferric phosphate. These won't harm other wildlife and they won't wash away in the first rain shower.
- Use barriers of copper, crushed egg shell, wood ash, bran, etc.
- Drown them in beer traps sunk into the soil.
- Stand pots above moats of water.

VINE WEEVIL grubs will eat through roots, causing plants to collapse. They are a particular problem for plants in pots and containers. The grubs are fat, C shaped, white and about 1cm/½in long. They are found in the compost or soil surrounding a plant. Strawberries in pots seem to be a particular favourite.

What can you do about vine weevil?

- Tip the contents of the pot out and shake the compost loose around the roots. The short fat grubs can be picked out and squashed.
- Remove any adult beetles if you find them.
- Use the biological control *Steinernema kraussei* to destroy the grubs.
- Prolonged periods above 28°C/82°F and below −2°C/28°F will kill grubs.

TOP: Ash and bran help keep slugs at bay
BOTTOM: Vine weevil grubs

WOODLICE, EARWIGS AND ANTS will all be present to a greater or lesser degree. Woodlice and earwigs will nibble seedlings and they can cut through stems. They make holes in the leaves of larger plants. Ants will 'farm' aphids in order to get the honeydew and so they help preserve a more damaging pest. Ants will also eat into strawberries, spoiling the fruit.

What can you do about woodlice, earwigs and ants?

- Stuff a jam jar with straw and turn this upside down on a stick. Earwigs will crawl up into the straw at night and can be removed during the day.
- Put a pile of decaying organic material on the ground. Woodlice will feed off this, but they will also hide underneath it during the day. Remove the pile a little at a time and collect the woodlice before they run away.
- Ants like dry soil. Soak everything and they will look for a drier place to make a nest.

Bird damage

BIRDS can be a help to the gardener. Some will eat insects and destroy lots of pests. However, birds can also be pests themselves. Blackbirds and starlings will squeeze under doors and peck through netting in order to get at ripe strawberries and grapes. Birds will also scratch about in the soil, burying seedlings and displacing mulch.

Pea seedlings
eaten by mice

What can you do about birds?

• Raise netting on hoops above strawberry pots. Weight it down well at the sides so that birds can't get underneath. You may lose one or two fruits if they are close to the netting, but most of the crop should survive.

• Hang netting across polytunnel doorways so that birds can't get in but fresh air can.

MICE AND RATS are a problem in the winter months. They seek a bit of shelter as the weather worsens and are always on the lookout for an easy source of food. Both rats and mice will dig up and eat pea and bean seeds, but they will also nip through the stems of these newly sprouted plants. All the young pea shoots might disappear overnight, only to be found hidden somewhere like in a pot or under a bit of polythene. A mouse will have made a store to feast on later and the potential pea crop will be lost.

What can you do about rats and mice?

• Get a cat!

• Set humane traps to catch them. Lethal traps might catch a cat instead of a rat.

• Poisoned bait will kill them, but please don't use this in the polytunnel. Rats will carry the poison and bury it, possibly in the compost heap, or somewhere close to an edible crop.

Rat damage

SOME POLYTUNNEL DISEASES

It can sometimes be hard to identify exactly which fungal disease is attacking a plant. Blotchy leaves and mouldy growths are common symptoms. However, the prevention and cure are often similar too. It's always best to try to get an accurate diagnosis, but it's better still to take action and deal with the problem as soon as it appears.

GREY MOULD (*BOTRYTIS*) will thrive in conditions where the humidity is high and ventilation is poor. It attacks a wide range of plants, including brassicas, strawberries, grapes, lettuce and tomatoes. The first signs can be a grey powdery dusting, or a soft rotting of leaves, fruit and stems. This will soon lead to a full fur-like growth of grey mould. If you wipe the mould away, you will find that the plant tissue underneath has begun to rot. If severely affected leaves are disturbed, a cloud of spores will rise like dust in the air. Stems can rot through and a whole plant be lost if grey mould does its worst. In tomatoes ghost spots are formed where spores of grey mould have dried on the fruit.

Grey mould right through a broccoli stem

What can you do about grey mould?
- Remove any affected leaves, fruit, etc. as soon as you notice the disease and before it spreads spores to other plants. Evict whole plants if necessary and don't shake them about on the way out!
- Keep the polytunnel ventilated.
- Interestingly enough, prolonged temperatures below 0°C/32°F seem to kill the mould, leaving a brown stain on the leaf where it once grew. A cold hard winter may go some way to freeing the polytunnel from the grip of this disease.

LEAF MOULD (*CLADOSPORIUM*) can be a particular problem with tomatoes. The first signs are yellow blotches on the leaves. These can run into one another as the disease spreads and the centre of the blotches may turn bright green. If you turn the leaf over, you may see a brownish mould growing underneath. Spores need high humidity and temperatures above 10°C/50°F to become active. The disease can be carried from one year to the next on plant debris or in the soil.

Grey mould on grapes

What can you do about leaf mould?
- Keep the polytunnel well ventilated through the summer months.
- Grow a *Cladosporium*-resistant variety of tomato, such as 'Shirley'.
- Rotate crops, so that tomatoes aren't grown in the same soil year on year.
- Clear and burn all debris after the crop is finished.
- Don't use seed from tomatoes that have been affected by this disease.
- Try not to splash water on the leaves of plants. However, if you are misting in order to ensure that the first trusses set fruit, do this early in the morning before temperatures rise.

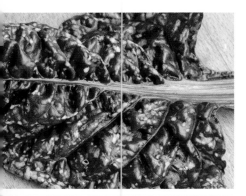

TOP: Leaf spot
BOTTOM: Powdery mildew

Potato blight

LEAF SPOT is a general term for several diseases. The origin could be fungal or viral. Spots present as soft, pale areas of dead tissue. The edges are clearly defined and often circular or oval. They might have a reddish ring around the outside; some appear pitted and some grow into one another until the whole leaf can be destroyed. Swiss chard, spinach and beetroot seem to be particularly prone to leaf spot during the winter months. It can make older leaves look unsightly, but it won't usually kill the plant.

What can you do about leaf spot?
• Remove affected leaves. These are usually the large, older ones. New growth can often be unaffected.
• Harvest regularly while leaves are small.

POWDERY MILDEW first shows itself as white spots on the surface of cucumber, melon, pumpkin and courgette leaves. The problem is usually a result of dry soil. Leaves can become totally coated in white fungal growth. Old leaves are usually the first to be affected, but growth will be stunted if the disease spreads over too much of the plant.

What can you do about powdery mildew?
• Correct watering regimes so that the soil doesn't dry out.
• Remove any severely affected leaves.
• Spray plants with a solution of one part milk to nine parts water. Repeat every day for a week and then every week after that.
• Grow a resistant or tolerant variety such as 'Burpless Tasty Green', 'Carmen' or 'Tiffany'.

BLIGHT is a serious fungal disease that affects both potatoes and tomatoes. Spores can blow into the polytunnel on damp misty days. Blight attack usually starts in July and can go on through the summer. Leaves show the first signs of the disease, with dark greyish blotches that spread in from the edge of the leaf. These can be large, are soft, have an irregular shape and will merge together to eventually blacken the whole leaf. Affected foliage has a distinctive mouldy smell. Blight will spread down potato stems to infect the tubers, which will rot. Tomato fruit will be ruined, with brown patches.

What can you do about blight?
• Polytunnel crops have some protection, since the spores have to find their way inside. On damp muggy days in the summer keep doors closed if possible.
• Remove any potato crops from the tunnel by mid-June at the absolute latest.

- Remove and burn any affected tomato leaves and fruit. Don't add these to the compost heap.
- Keep foliage dry as much as possible. Blight needs some moisture in order to take hold.
- Use a foliar liquid feed made from compost. The theory is that microorganisms in the compost compete with the blight spores.
- Grow a resistant tomato variety such as 'Ferline'.

GUMMOSIS is a fungal disease that particularly attacks cucumbers, but it may attack melons as well. Fruit has sunken grey sticky patches that ooze fluid. Spores will form in the patches, furthering the spread of this disease.

What can you do about gummosis?
- Remove any affected fruit.
- Ensure adequate ventilation.
- Keep temperatures above 20°C/68°F if possible.
- Grow a resistant variety of cucumber such as 'Melen'.

ROOT ROT can be caused by a variety of fungal or bacterial diseases. You may notice nothing untoward until plants start to wilt. In severe cases the plant can collapse and die in a short period of time. Cucumbers and melons are particularly susceptible to this disease. Young plants will collapse in pots and even large ones can flop overnight. Any plant can suffer from root rot if it is grown in waterlogged soil.

What can you do about root rot?
- Don't sow cucumbers until late March at the earliest.
- Make a second sowing of cucumbers in late April or May. These can replace any that you lose from earlier sowings.
- Keep compost damp but never wet. A slightly dry compost will do less harm than a soggy one.
- Avoid dramatic temperature swings when plants are in pots. Planting out into the border, a hotbed or a large pot will give a steadier temperature around the roots.
- Use a free-draining medium when planting out, or make a mound and plant into that.
- Pile compost up around the stem of growing cucumber and melon plants. Do this every couple of weeks to allow healthy, new roots to grow further up the stem.

DAMPING OFF affects small seedlings rather than large plants. Seedlings suddenly flop in their pots and the base of the stem shrivels where it goes into the compost. Damping off is a fungal disease, which is encouraged by overcrowding and overwatering. It can be spread through using dirty pots or unsterilized compost.

TOP: Blight on tomatoes
BOTTOM: Root rot on cucumber plant

TOP: Chamomile tea helps prevent damping off
BOTTOM: Strawberry leaf showing signs of virus disease

What can you do about damping off?

- Remove coverings from propagators on sunny days to allow air to circulate.
- Wash all previously used pots and add a disinfectant like Citrox to the washing water.
- Sterilize garden compost if it is to be used for raising sensitive seedlings (see Part 7).
- Chamomile tea might give some resistance to damping off.
- Don't overwater seedlings.

VIRUSES can affect most plants. The most common symptoms are discoloured or misshapen leaves. Viruses live within the cells of the plant and are often introduced through cuts and wounds. Aphids can carry viruses from one plant to another and inject the problem while they feed. Some plants tolerate virus diseases and still produce good crops. Others will never crop well once they show signs of disease. Strawberry plants raised from seed seem particularly susceptible to virus attack. Cucumber mosaic virus can lead to distortion of fruit and leaves. The whole plant may eventually collapse and die.

What can you do about virus disease?

- Prune or remove side shoots while the stems are tiny, making the smallest possible wound.
- Keep greenfly under control.
- Use a liquid foliar feed made from seaweed and compost. This strengthens the plant and makes it more resistant to disease.
- Try the milk spray used for powdery mildew. It will do no harm and seems to do some good.
- Remove any seriously affected plants.

Diluted milk helps fight powdery mildew

MINERAL DEFICIENCIES

Not all plant problems are due to pests and diseases. Mineral deficiencies might be to blame for symptoms that mimic those of disease. Deficiencies are present in many soils, even when added fertilizers are used. Excess of one mineral can lock up another one, making it unavailable to plant roots. Always look closely and try to determine exactly what the problem is. There might just be a quick fix.

TOP: Liquid manure combats nitrogen shortage
BOTTOM: Leaf showing magnesium shortage

Nitrogen

Small plants that show poor growth indicate a shortage of nitrogen. Leaves are often more yellow than green. Apply a nitrogen-rich feed like well-rotted or liquid manure.

An excess of nitrogen is indicated by plants that produce a mass of dark green leaves at the expense of flowers and fruit. Apply potash to try to lock up some of the excess.

Potassium (potash)

A shortage of potash is indicated initially by brown or yellow edges to leaves. This discolouration spreads in towards the midrib. The tops of the plants may be thin, and ripened tomatoes might have blotches of yellow and green. Poor growth and poor yields are common. Apply a potash-rich feed such as seaweed, or a sprinkling of wood ash.

Excess potash is indicated by the tops of plants browning at the growing points. Apply lime if necessary to reduce uptake of potash, or water soil well to try to wash away some of the excess.

Phosphorous

A shortage of phosphorous is indicated when leaves have a purple or reddish tinge. Plants can be small, stunted and prone to disease. Crops will be slow to mature. Apply rock phosphate or bonemeal to provide the missing mineral.

Magnesium

A shortage of magnesium will show as mottled leaves with dark veins and yellowing in between. This is particularly common in fast-growing polytunnel crops like cucumbers. Potash will lock up magnesium – especially on acid soils. Apply a solution of Epsom salts (two teaspoons in a watering can) for a quick fix. Repeat as necessary.

Calcium

A shortage of calcium will show as leaves that brown and start to die from the stem end up. Blossom end rot in tomatoes can be partly attributed to lack of calcium. Soils that are short of calcium will be acid and sour. Apply lime to rectify the problem.

SOME PHYSICAL PROBLEMS

Frost and low temperatures

The polytunnel should provide enough protection to keep frost off plants for most of the year. In an exceptionally cold winter, however, plants might freeze inside the polytunnel. To reduce damage, pour cool water over the frozen plants before the sun hits and temperatures start to rise. A sudden thaw will do the most damage.

Frosted tomato and pepper plants will usually wilt. Leaves may start to brown after a light frost, or turn black after a hard one.

Low temperatures can damage tender plants in the early months of the year. Newly planted tomato plants will survive temperatures as low as 3°C/37°F, but the leaves can become almost transparent and silvery, and the plants will never go on to crop to their full potential. Cover vulnerable plants with extra layers of fleece if temperatures are low.

Split fruit

More tomatoes split as the season progresses. Skins tend to be thinner in autumn fruit. Poor watering can also cause fruit to split, especially if you give a lot of water after having previously allowed the soil to dry out. In order to get sound fruit, water regularly and avoid extremes.

Dry set

The first truss of tomatoes may not set fruit. The same is true of peppers and aubergines. The answer is to lightly dampen the pollen by misting plants overhead with water. Spray in the morning and don't soak the plants. This only needs to be done for the first flowers; later ones seem to have fewer problems setting fruit.

Blossom end rot

The flower end of tomato fruit sometimes turns black, hard and dry. Applying lime to the soil is one solution to this problem, but lack of water can be another cause. Adjust watering regimes so that plants never go short.

RIGHT: Mist tomato flowers with water to avoid dry set OPPOSITE: Keep soil in good health for problem-free crops

6

ONGOING CARE

CROP ROTATION IN A POLYTUNNEL

The principle of crop rotation is simple: don't grow the same or a similar crop on the same piece of ground in consecutive years and, if possible, don't grow the same crop on the same piece of ground for another three or four years.

The practice is simple too: draw up a plan and stick to it.

Of course, you can add something new into the scheme at any time, as long as it rotates in the right family group along with all the cousins.

Why rotate crops?

- To reduce disease and pest problems. Vegetables that belong to the same family (see the lists below) tend to suffer from the same pests and diseases. Crop rotation won't solve all problems, especially in the small space of a polytunnel, but it is a good starting point in the battle. Obviously pests can hop from one part of the polytunnel to another, and soil-borne diseases can be trampled around on the bottom of boots, but crops that are rotated still fare better than ones that are grown on the same soil every year.

OPPOSITE:
Rotate crops in blocks
TOP: Draw up a plan
BOTTOM: Brassicas like an alkaline soil

- To provide the appropriate food for each crop. Some crops fare best in soil that was manured for the previous crop. Some, such as sweetcorn, are heavy feeders; others such as peas and beans don't need much nitrogen, since they make their own and leave it in the soil for the next crop to use. Carrots tend to fork if there is too much manure in the bed and brassicas do best on a firm soil not too rich in nitrogen. Each year's planting and feeding should improve the soil and leave it in good heart for what is to grow there next.

- To ensure acidity requirements are met. Brassicas like an alkaline soil, but tomatoes like an acid one. Hence it makes sense to lime the brassica patch, having planned that the tomatoes won't grow there for another three years, by which time a lot of the lime will have washed away.

- To get a balance between deep-rooted and shallow-rooted crops. Deep-rooting crops such as sweetcorn draw minerals up from lower layers of the soil. Lettuce feeds happily nearer the surface. Alternating deep and shallow feeders will ensure deep cultivation and improve the structure of the soil.

- To maximize weed control. Some crops, such as courgettes and pumpkins, are good weed suppressors and will effectively reduce the number of weeds in following years.

How many years in a rotation?

A four-year rotation is ideal – simply view the polytunnel as four quarters and move everything around clockwise, into the neighbouring quarter, each year. If the tunnel is divided into three long beds, a three-year rotation might make sense. In a small polytunnel it might only be possible to do a two-year rotation, unless you introduce containers and growbags to effectively include a third area into the scheme. Basically, anything is better than same crop, same soil, for year upon year.

Family ties

All vegetables fall into a family grouping and it is best to grow all of one family in the same bed and to rotate these crops together.

Squash and courgettes are part of the cucurbit family

- **Cabbage (brassica) family:** Cabbage, broccoli, kohl rabi, cauliflower, Brussels sprouts, turnips, kale, swede, radish, mizuna, rocket, mustard greens, etc.
- **Onion (allium) family:** Onion, leek, garlic, shallot, chive
- **Carrot (umbellifer) family:** Carrot, parsley, Florence fennel
- **Cucumber (cucurbit) family:** Cucumber, marrow, courgette, pumpkin, squash, melon, gourd
- **Pea and bean (legume) family:** Pea, broad bean, French bean, runner bean, soya bean
- **Potato (solanum) family:** Potato, tomato, pepper, aubergine
- **Goosefoot (*Chenopodiaceae*) family:** Swiss chard, spinach, spinach beet, beetroot (these often get mistaken for brassicas)
- *Asteraceae* **family:** Lettuce, endive
- **Corn (*Gramineae*) family:** Sweetcorn

A few tips

- Some crops, such as lettuce, spinach and sweetcorn, don't belong to the major families and can be fitted in almost anywhere where space allows.
- Keep planting on a year-round basis to fill gaps, but try to make sure the new planting is part of the planned rotation scheme.
- Remember, nothing is written in stone. It is often better to fill a gap than to leave it empty, and it is also better to tweak the plan as the years go by. The aim is to use the polytunnel to its full potential.
- Pots, growbags and containers can be moved around as desired, particularly if these don't allow plants to root down into the border soil.

A sample plan

Tomatoes Aubergines Peppers	P A T H	Cucumbers Melons Pumpkins (and hence sweetcorn) Courgettes
Kohl rabi Spinach Mizuna Rocket Lettuce Broccoli Cabbage Beetroot		Peas Beans Herbs Strawberries

This plan will rotate one-quarter clockwise in the following year.

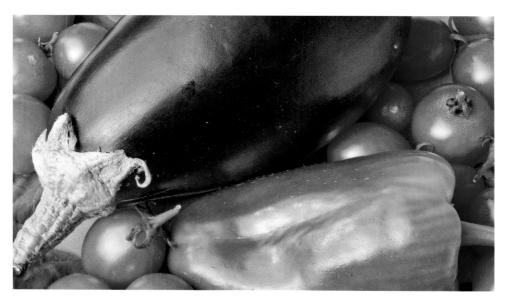

All in the same family

TEN STEPS TO SOIL HEALTH

Polytunnels tend to be cultivated intensively; huge crops are expected from a small space and overcrowding can be the rule. All this puts strain on the soil, but there are solutions that can improve matters, short of the huge task of removing all soil and importing a fresh batch.

It's best to keep soil in good health on an ongoing basis rather than waiting for the signs of exhausted soil, or a disease problem that has got out of hand.

TOP: Compost tea
BOTTOM: Seaweed is great for
soil health

1. Practise crop rotation, as outlined on the previous page. Just a little planning will give plants a better chance.

2. When removing crops, try to clear all debris and leave soil completely bare. One squashed tomato can produce a batch of seedlings that will carry disease forward into a new crop. Gather up all dried and diseased leaves and pull up roots. Don't cherish legume roots in the polytunnel, even though they may add a little nitrogen.

3. Allow as much sunlight as possible into the structure, as this can have a cleansing effect. Wash down the inside of the polythene with a dilute Citrox solution to kill off spores without harming plants. Remember that the frame also needs scrubbing down.

4. Add manure and compost. Both of these provide an obvious nutrient boost and help restore depleted soils. Dig in manure in the autumn, so that it has time to break down completely before you plant spring and summer crops. Compost contains microbes which compete with organisms in the soil that are responsible for some plant diseases. You can make compost tea by adding a shovelful of compost to a bucketful of water. Stir well and leave this to stand overnight before pouring it on to the soil. Water the whole soil's surface in this way, if possible.

5. Add some seaweed to cleanse the soil. Use fresh seaweed as a mulch, make a liquid feed or scatter powdered meal over the surface of the soil. Fresh seaweed appears to have the perfect balance of minerals, nutrients and microorganisms needed to help restore depleted and diseased soils. Seaweed can be bought as a powder or a concentrated liquid. Both of these will be of great nutritional benefit, although they obviously don't have the same microbial action as the fresh weed.

6. Alternate drought and flooding to confuse bugs. Allow empty borders to completely dry out. Leave them this way for two weeks, and then flood to saturation point. Repeat this process at intervals over the winter months. Few inactive pests and diseases can tolerate such extremes, especially if the top layer of soil gets powder dry. Earthworms will be safe enough, since they move to deeper levels in the soil or simply shift sideways to a better spot. This is not a cure-all, but it helps!

   Seawater can work miracles if the state of the soil is really bad. Use this to flood the soil instead of water from the tap.

7. Keep the surface of the soil moving. During the cold wet months of the year, soil can develop a green crust. Keep hoeing to break this up. Aeration of the soil's surface is a very old rule of gardening. It used to be called 'tickling the soil' and is of real benefit in combating the stagnant conditions that can develop in a polytunnel.

8. Encourage wildlife! Frogs eat a variety of pests, as do ground beetles. Thank heavens for ladybirds and hoverflies! Don't indiscriminately kill all living things just because it's hard to tell which ones are friends and which are foes.

9. Choose disease-resistant varieties. Search in the organic sections of seed catalogues: there are varieties bred for all kinds of resistance to disease. Growing these will help break the cycle and will reduce the build-up of problems in the soil.

10. Buy a soil tonic such as Revive, Garden N or Rootgrow. These are packed full of microorganisms to help plants grow better even in a poor soil.

TOP: Tickle the soil
BOTTOM: Frogs are friends and should be encouraged

REPAIRS & MAINTENANCE

How to make polythene last more than a decade
- Buy the best-grade polythene available.
- Plant a hedge, put up a fence or use strong netting to create a windbreak. This doesn't have to be so high that it shades the polytunnel, but it does have to be high enough to deflect strong winds.
- Buy a roll of repair tape at the same time as buying the polytunnel. Use this to repair small holes and rips before they become large ones.
- Check the polythene regularly.
- Remove any overhanging branches before they fall and damage the polythene. A tree surgeon might be needed to do this.
- If a strong wind blows in at one door of the polytunnel, either close it or open another door so that the wind can get out again.

Polytunnel repair kit

How to repair rips and holes
Even new polythene can tear or be punctured, but if you repair a small hole straight away it won't develop into a rip. Repair tape, which looks like a giant roll of Sellotape, will do a much more effective job than duck tape (also called duct tape), parcel tape or masking tape. Buy the broadest roll available; it might seem expensive, but one roll will last a long time. Check the polythene cover every few weeks, especially through the winter months and after strong winds. If a sharp stick or fork pokes a hole, repair it straight away. If you catch damage while it is still small, you can do a good repair job in six easy steps:

1. Wash the polythene inside and out around the tear. Use soapy water for this (washing-up liquid works well) and a kitchen sponge with a mild abrasive pad to remove any film of dirt.
2. Dry the polythene with a piece of kitchen roll and leave it to air dry completely before applying a patch. If in a hurry, use a hair dryer.
3. Cut a length of tape that will cover the rip with a minimum of 2cm/¾in overlap all around.
4. Cut the points off the four corners of the repair patch. This makes the edge less likely to lift and peel away.
5. Enlist a helper to support the back of the polythene. Apply firm steady pressure while pressing the patch into place. Remove any air bubbles by squeezing them toward an edge of the patch. Make sure you achieve a tight bond all around.
6. Swap sides and repeat, so that you patch the damage both inside and out.

☑ You can repair larger rips using the same principle, but you may need several helpers to support the polythene.

How to clean a polytunnel

1. Add some Citrox (or Citricidal), plus a squirt of environmentally safe washing-up liquid, to a bucket or bowl of warm water.
2. Start with the outside and, using a small brush, scrub out any folds that might harbour pests and diseases.
3. Next use a long-handled broom with soft bristles to scrub down the polythene. Make sure the brush is the right size to dip into the bucket or bowl. Refill the bucket with soapy water as often as necessary.
4. To reach over the top of a tall structure, use a soft brush head fitted on to the end of a hosepipe – these are often used for washing cars. You can extend the length of 'reach' by taping the brush to a long smooth stick or a telescopic handle. Take care that there are no protruding parts that might tear the polythene. Clear water running through the pipe will be perfectly fine for cleaning over the top – just scrub a little with the brush.
5. Use a hosepipe to rinse the polythene with clear water.
6. Repeat the process on the inside of the tunnel, but remember to wear a waterproof jacket with the hood up! The long-handled brush should reach to the top, but it will drip.
7. Give any growing plants a quick squirt of clean water.
8. Stand back to admire the effect, but also to check for any bits that you have missed.

Wash down the plastic to keep light levels high

Repairing doors

Galvanized metal doors will last for years, although they might need re-covering with polythene. Wooden ones might fall apart and rot. If a new wooden door is needed, it isn't hard to make one. Don't use heavy timber, as this might pull on the frame (47mm x 22mm is fine). Do use diagonal bracing so that the door doesn't twist or slip out of shape. A diagonal brace can be as simple as a piece of timber running from one corner to the diagonally opposite one. Make sure the corners are square before screwing the brace in place. Alternatively, triangles of plywood can be screwed across each corner.

Check hinges to see if these need to be replaced. Screws can pull loose from the door frame.

Check the door catch at the same time. If it's loose, the door might blow open in a strong wind.

Repair doors

7

MAKE YOUR OWN

HOW TO MAKE A HOTBED

If you want to take some of the uncertainty out of when to plant out tender crops like melons and cucumbers into an unheated polytunnel, try making a hotbed. This will keep plants warm even if night temperatures fall. Provided you can get hold of some fresh manure, making a hotbed really isn't a difficult task.

Preparation

Start preparing a hotbed about a week before the plants need to be planted out. Hotbeds deserve their name: they can build up terrific heat and it's best to allow some of this to disperse before introducing the roots of young plants.

Use fresh manure to build the bed, and if you can get hold of straw-based horse manure so much the better. Make this into a pile, add leaves or extra straw if you need to bulk it out and cover it with polythene. After three days turn the pile over to release some of the heat and to move some of the colder edges in to the warmer centre. Leave for another three days before making the bed.

Making a hotbed

1. Hotbeds can be made as freestanding mounds or, to take up less space, they can be put into a wooden frame. A frame that measures 45 x 120cm/18in x 4ft, and is 30cm/12in deep, will provide a comfortable home for three cucumber plants. The woodwork doesn't have to be sophisticated, as long as the structure doesn't fall apart.
2. Put the frame where the plants are to grow. Under a polytunnel hoop is ideal – this makes it easy to attach support strings. Make sure the frame is level and solid on the ground.
3. Dig out a 15cm/6in depth of soil from the bottom of the frame and pile this to one side. It will be used later to go back on top of the bed.
4. Put a layer of manure 30cm/12in deep in the base of the frame. If the manure is dry, sprinkle water over it. If the manure contains a lot of straw and you feel that there may not be enough dung, it can be useful to add urine at this stage. In fact, if fresh manure is not available, straw can be used on its own as the base of a hotbed – provided it is soaked in urine. This could be the time to invest in a chamber pot!
5. Put the soil that was removed at step 3 on top of the manure – or, preferably, use a mix of soil and compost. Don't fill the frame up to the rim, as space will be needed to earth up plants and to water the bed.

OPPOSITE: A hotbed gives tender plants an early start BELOW: Put a layer of manure in the base of the frame

Using the hotbed

- Wait a day or two before planting into the bed. This allows time for everything to settle and for heat to start to build up. Once the soil temperature has stabilized, you can put young plants directly into the soil; or you can dig out a hole and fill this with compost before planting out.

- If nights are cold after you have put plants in the bed, drape a layer of fleece over the top to form a tent. Remove this during the day so that air can circulate.
- Heat is generated as the straw and manure decompose. This process does not go on indefinitely, but there should be a good three or four weeks of extra heat for the young plants.
- Hotbeds provide a free-draining root run, but it's important to water regularly so that roots don't dry out.
- Hotbeds can also be used to give a boost of heat to winter crops.

Cucumbers grow rapidly in a hotbed

HOW TO MAKE YOUR OWN POTTING MIXES

If you have a compost heap and, better still, if it heats up to produce a dark, friable material, you are on the way to producing some excellent potting mixtures. Dig down into the heart of the heap and extract really well-rotted compost. This is where the highest temperatures will be and hence the compost is less likely to contain weed seeds or disease spores. You can use this material straight from the heap for larger plants in containers. However, if you want to make a more sophisticated mix, consider adding some of the following ingredients.

Leafmould is the dense, dark material that is formed when leaves decompose. If you own a deciduous woodland, you can dig deep through the layers of leaves on the forest floor until you find the dark, rich mould at the base of it all. Most people don't own woodlands and the most environmentally sound alternative is to pile up autumn leaves and let them rot for a year or two; it takes at least this long to make really fine leafmould. This is a useful addition to home-made potting mixes. It absorbs water and so keeps the mix damp.

A leafmould bin

Compost from a wormery is too rich for most seed mixtures, although it is fine for use with larger plants.

Seaweed powder is great in any potting mix. Seaweed has a good range of trace elements and is very high in potash. Use one teaspoon per bucketful in mixtures for raising seeds. Increase the amount to two tablespoons per bucketful for potting on large plants.

Comfrey leaves should be chopped (wear gloves, as you may get a rash) and put in a black polythene bag. Ideally use alternate layers of comfrey and leafmould. The contents should be just damp rather than wet. Seal the bag and leave for two to five months before using.

Charcoal has a pH of 8–9 and will 'sweeten' an acid mix. It will also help to improve moisture retention in the compost. Always use activated (steam-treated) charcoal.

Sand plays a role in most mixes. It helps create air spaces and hence improves drainage. Sharp sand, or silver sand, is usually recommended, but try some building sand first. Rub a bit between your finger and thumb: if it feels silky, it's no use; if it feels gritty and 'sharp', it's probably OK. Sand from the seaside will have a high salt content, which isn't ideal for seedlings.

Rotted cow manure can be used in potting mixes

Perlite and **vermiculite** are natural materials and are acceptable in organic mixtures. They are pH neutral, help improve drainage and will hold three to four times their weight in water. If sand and leafmould are in short supply, perlite or vermiculite will make a good addition to a mix based on dense garden compost or loam.

Manure must be rotted down before use. Cow manure, with organic straw, is one of the best for using in potting mixes. Goat, pig and horse manure are also good, but slightly more concentrated in nutrients. Poultry and pigeon manure can be too strong for potting mixes and certainly shouldn't be used in the proportions given in the following recipes – a small sprinkling goes a long way. Manure gives a nitrogen boost to any mix. Apply it sparingly; otherwise it may lock up other trace elements. Never use more than one-third manure in a mix, even for the greediest plants.

Garden soil can dry out in a pot to form a concrete-like mass. This doesn't mean garden soil shouldn't be used, but do follow a few rules:
- Dig soil from a fertile part of the garden, which has a good humus balance.
- Don't use soil where disease has been a problem, unless you intend to sterilize it.
- Never use more than two-thirds soil and balance this with leafmould, or a sand and leafmould mix.
- Soil from a molehill can make excellent loam for use in potting mixes – a great way of turning a pest to your advantage.

Lime or wood ashes will raise pH.

Coir fibre is quite acidic and can be used instead of leafmould to lower pH.

Finely shredded newspaper will hold water and can be used if that's all you have got.

Sawdust will also hold water, but if you use it you run the risk of it robbing nitrogen from the mix as it rots.

Fish, blood and bonemeal will provide nutrients.

Tips and techniques when making potting mixes
- Use a riddle to sieve home-made compost. This will remove any large chunks of material and any wildlife.
- Small quantities of compost can be sterilized in an oven (80°C/180°F/Gas mark ½ or S on some cookers) for about one hour, or in the microwave (if sieved and contained in a plastic bag). Large quantities can be spread on a piece of flat metal over an open fire, or you can use a flame weeding device to apply direct heat.
- Mix small quantities in a bucket. For larger amounts use a wheelbarrow.
- Make sure the mix is damp enough before storing it in strong plastic sacks.
- Follow a recipe to make sure minerals aren't locked up by an imbalance of materials.

Recipes for starting seeds

1 part compost
2 parts fine leafmould
1 part sharp sand

Or:
1 part good loam (if the loam is very heavy add a little perlite)
1 part leafmould
1 part sharp sand

Recipes for potash-greedy plants like tomatoes

1 part compost
1 part sharp sand
2 tablespoons seaweed meal per bucketful of potting mix

Or:
1 part leafmould
1 part chopped comfrey leaves

Comfrey

NOTE: This mix doesn't provide nutrients for long and you will need to use a liquid feed after four to six weeks, or top up the containers with more compost.

High-nitrogen and water-retaining recipes for larger plants in containers

1 part leafmould
1 part well-rotted manure
1 part compost
1 part perlite

Or:
3 parts loam
2 parts leafmould
1 part well-rotted manure
1 part sharp sand

Recipe for drought-sensitive plants

8 parts compost
2 parts charcoal

The charcoal controls the availability of water in the mix.

HOW TO MAKE LIQUID FEEDS

There is a myth that liquid feeds are difficult to prepare and that they take a long time to be ready for use. This couldn't be further from the truth. All you need is a container, material from which to prepare the feed and a small bit of patience. If you don't have any suitable manure, don't worry – there are other things that you can use. Some feeds can be ready for use in a couple of days; others may take two or three weeks.

Goat manure has a good balance of nitrogen and potassium

Liquid manures

Cow manure is the lowest in nitrogen, phosphate and potassium of all the common animal manures, but it may well be the easiest to acquire. Horse and goat manure both have a good balance of nitrogen and potassium, which will boost leaf, root and fruit growth. You can also make liquid manure from rabbit droppings.

WARNING: Don't even consider using cat or dog faeces.

1. Fill a small sack, or permeable bag, with animal manure – a generous half-bucketful is about right for using with a 180-litre/40-gallon container. If you are using poultry manure, use only a quarter of a bucketful to this size of container. Try to avoid incorporating too much straw or other bedding material – it will do no harm, but the liquid manure will be less concentrated.

2. Tie the top of the bag, using one end of a piece of strong twine. Tie the other end of the twine to a stout stick. The stick shouldn't bend when the bag is suspended from it and it must be long enough to rest across the top of the container. A dustbin or plastic barrel is an ideal container, but you can use a bucket if you require only a small amount, scaling down the amount of manure appropriately.

3. Suspend the bag of manure in the container and then fill with water. If your container is to be kept outdoors, the top must be covered. I use a dustbin lid, with an elasticated 'bungee' strap to hold it in place. You can even use a large square of polythene with a stone tied to each corner. It's essential that rain can't get in but that you can gain easy access.

Suspend the bag of manure in the container

4. Poke the bag gently with a stick, or swirl it around occasionally, to help release nutrients into the water.

5. The liquid will be ready to start using within a couple of days, but it will get stronger if left for two or three weeks. It should be diluted with an equal quantity of plain water (until it looks like weak tea) and can then be poured directly around any vigorously growing crop.

6. As you use the liquid, you can add more water to the container. Keep poking and moving the bag of manure from time to time. This releases as much goodness as possible. Eventually, as more liquid is used and replaced, the manure in the bag will become exhausted. At this point the liquid will be quite light in colour

and won't need any dilution before use. At that point remove the bag of manure and either add the contents to the compost heap or use them as a mulch.

Comfrey and stinging nettles

These are both rich in minerals and make excellent liquid feeds. A bed of comfrey can be cut two or three times a year and nettles can be cut twice. Make sure you wear gloves to avoid skin irritation and try to cut before the plants start to flower.

Wear thick gloves when cutting nettles

1. Cut the nettle or comfrey stems about 5cm/2in above the ground.
2. Allow the leaves to wilt overnight.
3. The next day, pack the cut herb into a dustbin or barrel, pressing down firmly but not packing it solid.
4. Completely cover the plants with water and fit a lid on the container. You can draw liquid off after the first week, but it will reach full strength after three weeks. The leaves will be almost fully digested at this point, although the stems will take much longer to break down.
5. The diluted liquid can be watered around plants or used as a foliar spray. If you intend to spray, it's worth filtering the liquid through a fine sieve, so that small bits of plant debris don't clog the sprayer nozzle.
6. When the container is emptied, any sludge remaining in the bottom makes excellent feed for tomatoes and peppers.

☑ An autumn cut of comfrey will make a brew to last through the winter. This can be used to give a boost to overwintered crops.

Urine

Urine is a ready-made liquid feed. Dilute it with twice the amount of pure water before use. Apply this around the roots of tomato plants for prolific crops. Ailing plants will often revive with this treatment. Don't forget that urine added to your compost heap is an excellent activator!

Seaweed

Liquid seaweed concentrates are available commercially. It makes sense to buy an organic one and always dilute according to the instructions on the pack. Nothing is gained by making too strong a mix.

If you have access to fresh seaweed, you can make your own liquid feed. A bucketful of seaweed (washed up above the high-tide line and never pulled from the rocks) is all that you need.

Fresh seaweed makes an excellent liquid feed

1. Rinse fresh seaweed with clear water to remove any excess sand and salt.
2. Fill the container with water, so that the seaweed is covered, and

leave the brew to stand. The seaweed will soon start to break down.

3. Stir every couple of days and start to draw off the liquid when it turns dark brown.

4. This is a high-potash feed. Dilute it with equal amounts of fresh water before using around peppers, aubergines and tomatoes.

☑ Ailing plants of all kinds perk up when fed with liquid seaweed and it is always worth trying this remedy before giving up on any plant.

NOTE: Seaweed makes an excellent foliar feed.

Cold black tea is the simplest liquid feed

Tea
Allow any unused tea to cool before adding it to pot-grown plants or growbags. You can also add used tea leaves or bags to any other bin where you are brewing a liquid feed.

A few general tips for using liquid feeds
• Most liquid feeds will be ready for use after a week, but they gain full strength after three or four weeks. If you are in a hurry, you can draw some liquid off after three days.
• A full-strength brew should be diluted with equal parts of water before application.
• Never apply liquid feeds to small seedlings.
• Don't apply liquid feeds to dry soil.
• As you draw liquid off from the container, keep adding more water to top it up. Stop adding more water when the brew is the colour of weak tea.
• Try to keep one tub of liquid feed available at all times. Or better still, have two or three bins with different brews for use throughout the year.

Dilute home-made brews until they are the colour of weak tea

LIST OF SUPPLIERS

POLYTUNNELS
UK
Citadel Polytunnels, www.citadelpolytunnels.com
tel: 01789 842689
Ferryman Polytunnels, www.ferryman.uk.com
tel: 01363 83444
First Tunnels (instruction DVD),
www.firsttunnels.co.uk tel: 01282 601253
Five Star Polytunnels, www.polytunnels.me.uk
tel: 01570 421580
Growing Spaces (domes), www.growingspaces.co.uk
tel: 07941 473680
Haygrove (side vents), www.gardentunnels.co.uk
tel: 08452696395
Keder (v. strong bubble polythene),
www.kedergreenhouse.co.uk tel: 01386 49094
Knowle Nets, www.knowlenets.co.uk
tel: 01308 424342
Northern Polytunnels,
www.northernpolytunnels.co.uk tel: 01282 873120
Solar Tunnels (mesh), www.solartunnels.co.uk
tel: 01903 742615
Pidley Polydomes, www.polydomes.co.uk
tel: 01487841946
Premier Polytunnels, www.premierpolytunnels.co.uk
tel: 01282 811250

IRELAND
Colm Warren Polyhouses, www.cwp.ie
tel: 046 9546007
Fruit Hill Farm (also organic garden supplies),
www.fruithillfarm.com tel: 027 50710
Highbank, www.highbank.ie tel: 056 7729918
Polydome, www.polydome.ie tel: 057 9120424
Polytunnels Ireland, www.polytunnelsireland.ie
tel: 087 9800687

GARDEN SUPPLIES
(cloches, fleece, benches, watering, propagators, etc.)
Ferndale, www.ferndale-lodge.co.uk
tel: 0844 314 0043
Harrod Horticultural, www.harrodhorticultural.com
tel: 0845 402 5300
Haxnicks, www.haxnicks.co.uk
tel: 0845 241 1555
Two Wests & Elliott, www.twowests.co.uk
tel: 01246 451077

PEST CONTROLS
Copperbed, www.copperbed.co.uk tel: 0845 2252118
Citrox, www.citrox.net tel: 01642 241777
Green Gardener, www.greengardener.co.uk
tel: 01493 750061

Nemasys, www.nemasysinfo.com
See also: The Organic Gardening Catalogue, Unwins,
Fruit Hill Farm, etc.

SEED AND PLANT CATALOGUES
(some of these also sell garden supplies)
UK
The Organic Gardening Catalogue,
www.OrganicCatalogue.com tel: 01932 253666
Thompson & Morgan, www.thompson-morgan.com
tel: 0844 5731818
Dobies, www.dobies.co.uk
tel: 0844 7017625
D.T. Brown, www.dtbrownseeds.co.uk
tel: 0845 3710532
Kings, www.kingsseeds.com (www.kingsplants.co.uk)
tel: 01376 570000
Mr Fothergill's, www.mr-fothergills.co.uk
tel: 0845 3710518
Ken Muir (fruit), www.kenmuir.co.uk
tel: 01255 830181
Marshalls, www.marshalls-seeds.co.uk
tel: 01480 443390
Suffolk Herbs, www.suffolkherbs.com
tel: 01376 572456
Simply Vegetables, www.plantsofdistinction.co.uk
tel: 01449 721720
Sutton's Seeds, www.suttons.co.uk
tel: 0844 9220606
Johnsons Seeds, www.johnsons-seeds.com
tel: 08456589147
Tamar Organics, www.tamarorganics.co.uk
tel: 01579 371087
Unwins, www.unwins.co.uk tel: 01480 443395
Heritage Seed Library, www.gardenorganic.org.uk
tel: 02476 303517

IRELAND
The Organic Centre, www.theorganiccentre.ie
tel: 07198 54343
Chase Organics, www.deelish.ie tel: 028 21374
Mr Middleton, www.mrmiddleton.com
tel: 01 8603674
Irish Seed Savers, www.irishseedsavers.ie
tel: 061 921866
Brown Envelope Seeds,
www.brownenvelopeseeds.com tel: 028 38184

USEFUL ADDRESSES
Garden Organic, www.gardenorganic.org.uk
tel: 024 7630 3517
The Soil Association, www.soilassociation.org
tel: 0117 314 5000
The Royal Horticultural Society, www.rhs.org.uk
tel: 0845 260 5000

GLOSSARY

Bolt
A plant is said to bolt when it tries to flower and set seed. This is usually a premature action.

Cells
These are trays divided into several sections, used for sowing seeds.

Cut-and-come-again
This usually refers to varieties of salad leaves where more leaves will grow after the first ones are harvested. Plants can be repeatedly cut or picked.

Drill
This is a depression made in the ground in which seeds can be sown. It will usually be 1–2cm/½–¾in deep and in a straight line marked with sticks and string.

Earthing up
This is the action of piling soil around the stem of a plant. It usually applies to potatoes, but the technique is also used with cucumbers and melons.

Harden off
Plants should be slowly acclimatized to growing in lower temperatures than those in which they have been raised. This process is called 'hardening off'. It can take several days.

In situ
Seed is sown *in situ* when it is sown directly into the ground where the plants will remain.

Mist
To 'mist' leaves and plants is to damp them with a fine spray of water.

pH
This is a measure of acidity and alkalinity. A neutral soil is pH 7. Above this is alkaline, below it is acid.

Root-trainers
These are special long cells used for raising long-rooted seedlings.

INDEX

Figures in **bold** refer to main entries.

ACKNOWLEDGEMENTS

Keder and Haygrove polytunnel manufacturers for pictures on pages 16 and 17
First Tunnels for providing DVDs
Rod Calder-Potts at Highbank Polytunnels for advice
Brídín Ashe, Christine Brewer, Fred LaHaye, Greg Woods, Gerd and Renate Neubek, for allowing us to photograph their polytunnels
Brendan Lyons for helping out with photography for pages 20 and 21
Gloria Greenwood for providing the index